NEW YORK REVIEW BOOKS
CLASSICS

T0032248

THE BIBLE AND POETRY

SIR MICHAEL EDWARDS was born near London in 1938 and educated at Christ's College, Cambridge, of which he is an Honorary Fellow. He writes in both English and French and is the author of many books of poetry and scholarly monographs, including *Towards a Christian Poetics*, *Of Making Many Books*, and *Racine et Shakespeare*. A longtime professor of English and comparative literature at the University of Warwick, he was made a chair at the Collège de France in 2002 and, in 2013, became the first English person ever to be elected to a seat at the Académie Française.

STEPHEN E. LEWIS teaches and writes about literature, philosophy, and Christian experience. He has translated books by several contemporary French phenomenologists, including Jean-Louis Chrétien, Jean-Luc Marion, and Claude Romano.

THE BIBLE AND POETRY

MICHAEL EDWARDS

Translated from the French by
STEPHEN E. LEWIS

NEW YORK REVIEW BOOKS

New York

THIS IS A NEW YORK REVIEW BOOK
PUBLISHED BY THE NEW YORK REVIEW OF BOOKS
207 East 32nd Street, New York, NY 10016
www.nyrb.com

Copyright © 2016 by Éditions de Fallois
Translation copyright © 2023 by Stephen E. Lewis
All rights reserved.

This work received support for excellence in publication and translation from Albertine Translation, a program created by Villa Albertine and funded by FACE Foundation.

Library of Congress Cataloging-in-Publication Data
Names: Edwards, Michael, 1938– author. | Lewis, Stephen E. (Stephen Evarts), translator.
Title: The Bible and poetry / by Michael Edwards; translated by Stephen E. Lewis.
Other titles: Bible et poésie. English
Description: New York: New York Review Books, [2022] | Series: New York Review Books classics | Translation of: Bible et poésie. | Includes bibliographical references. |
Identifiers: LCCN 2021050254 (print) | LCCN 2021050255 (ebook) | ISBN 9781681376370 (paperback) | ISBN 9781681376387 (ebook)
Subjects: LCSH: Hebrew poetry, Biblical—History and criticism. | Bible as literature. | Bible—Language, style.
Classification: LCC BS536 .E3913 2022 (print) | LCC BS536 (ebook) | DDC 221.6/6—dc23/eng/20211221
LC record available at https://lccn.loc.gov/2021050254
LC ebook record available at https://lccn.loc.gov/2021050255

ISBN 978-1-68137-637-0
Available as an electronic book; ISBN 978-1-68137-638-7

Printed in the United States of America on acid-free paper.
10 9 8 7 6 5 4 3 2 1

CONTENTS

STRANGE CHRISTIANITY

I.

WE DO NOT read the Bible as it is meant to be read. Theology always risks leading us astray by elaborating its own discourse, with the biblical texts merely as a point of departure. The presence of poetry in the Bible is the key to a more pertinent and more faithful reading. Such are the convictions that lead me to write this book.

There are many poems found in the Bible. We know this, vaguely and without giving it too much thought; but shouldn't we be rather astonished by the role of poetry in a collection of books with such a pressing and salutary word to express? And shouldn't we ask ourselves if the presence of this writing, so much more self-conscious and desirous than prose of a form it can make vibrate, affects the biblical "message" and changes its nature?

It is unsurprising that the Psalms are poems, given their liturgical purpose and the abyss of individual and collective emotions that they explore. At the heart of the Bible and yet also apart from it, they lay out, we might suppose, for both the individual and the community the lived experience of religion that other biblical books have the task of defining. We can accept the Song of Songs as a love poem, Jeremiah's Lamentations as a sequence of elegies, Job as a verse drama, and we discover without too much surprise a considerable number of poems in the historical books: the song of Moses and Myriam, for example, in Exodus 15; the canticle of Deborah and Barak in Judges 5; the lament of David for Saul and Jonathan in 2 Samuel 1. And yet when we think about the presence of all these poetic books in a work in which we expect to find doctrines, and the turn to poetry in so many of the historical books, it gives us reason to think again. And how should we react to Proverbs, where wisdom itself is taught in a poetic form? Or to the prophetic books, where poetry is sovereign, where warnings of the greatest urgency, for us as well as for the writers' contemporaries, come forth in verse?

Isn't this curious? And poetry appears from the beginning. In the second chapter of Genesis (verse 23), Adam welcomes the creation of woman in this way:

> Here at last the bone of my bones,
> and flesh of my flesh.
> This one shall be called woman,
> for she was drawn forth from man.

These are the very first human words reported; it is tempting and perhaps legitimate to draw some conclusions. By this point Adam has already named the animals, but the author only indicates this without recording the spoken words; in the world of the beginning, from which the author knows himself as well as his readers to be excluded, he probably recognized that there must have existed an intimate relationship between language and the real, between words and things, that we are incapable of regaining. But when Adam does speak for the first time, he is given an "Edenic" language, which our fallen languages can still attain in certain moments: thus Adam literally draws woman, *'ishah*, from man, *'ish*. Hebrew, thanks to the pleasure it takes in wordplay—in the ludic and deeply serious harmonies between the sounds of words and the beings, objects, ideas, and emotions to which they open themselves—is a language particularly and providentially skillful at suggesting what would be a cordial relation between our language and our world and a meaningful relation among the presences of the real. It is skillful in affirming the gravity of the lightest among the figures of rhetoric: the pun. Most important, as soon as the first man opens his mouth, he speaks in verse. Did the author think that in the world of primitive wonder language was naturally poetic? Is this why Adam, immediately after eating the forbidden fruit, responds to God in prose: "I heard your steps in the garden, and I was afraid because I was naked, and I hid myself" (Genesis 3:10)? We cannot know, but that first brief, spontaneous poem of Adam, which we seem to hear from so far away and from so close, solicits our attention and calls for our thought. If the language from before the Fall was poetic, or produced poems at moments charged with meaning, does poetry represent for us the apogee of our fallen speaking, its beginning and its end, its nostalgia and its hope?

In paging through Genesis, a book of history and not a collection of poems, we encounter an impressive number of poems. It is in poetry that God gives the law on murder and its punishment (Genesis 9:6), that Rebecca's family blesses her (24:60), that Isaac prophesies the future of Esau (27:39–40), and that Jacob blesses the twelve tribes of Israel (49:2–27). Given the occasional difficulty in identifying which passages are in verse, it may be that others will be discovered. The Bible de Jérusalem (I am reading from the 2009 edition) presents God as speaking several times in poetry in the first three chapters, beginning with the creation of man, as the Word of God gives birth to the only creature endowed with speech:

> God created man in his image,
> in the image of God he created him,
> man and woman he created them.

In approaching the Bible's beginning, we must often change our listening, our rhythm, our mode of attention and of being, in order to understand and receive a different language.

There are fewer poems in the New Testament, but they give even more food for thought. The Gospel of Luke introduces, from its first chapters, three poems: the canticles of Mary, Zachariah, and Simeon. Thus the Savior's life begins under the sign of poetry. The book of

Revelation, at the end of the Bible, contains additional canticles, as well as lamentations on Babylon, in poetry that appeals to the visionary imagination. In the name of Christianity, it returns to the *extravagant* poetry of the prophets. The first letter of John develops its thought with such felicity of rhythmic phrasing and close-crafted form that the Jerusalem Bible translates it completely in verse. These same translators have Paul's letter to the Romans begin and end in verse, thus using poetry to frame a doctrinal exposition animated by an inflamed but in principle "prosaic" process of reflection, analysis, and synthesis. Scholarly consensus also holds that the very same Paul opens his letters to the Ephesians and to the Colossians with hymns of the early church or of his own composition, another of which figures in the second chapter of the letter to the Philippians. Fragments of hymns also appear in his two letters to Timothy.

And let us also not forget that the New Testament is sprinkled with innumerable other poetic passages that are quoted from the Old Testament. Above all we note that Jesus himself seems at certain moments to speak in verse, as in the Beatitudes (Matthew 5, Luke 6) and the Lord's Prayer (Matthew 6, Luke 11). For the Jerusalem Bible, the Gospel of John, which begins with a long poem and in which John the Baptist on two occasions speaks in verse (1:30, 3:27–30), suggests that Jesus the teacher—or rather, the divine educator—addressed his listeners most often in poetry.

It is true that the border between verse and a cadenced prose is not easy to determine in either the Hebrew of the Old Testament or the Greek of the New: translators judge it differently. It may also be that the poems spoken by Jacob, Simeon, and many others come not from them, but from the authors of the books in which they appear. Even so, whether it is verse or prose divisible into sound units, whether the poem is the work of the historical (or mythical) character or of the writer, the result is the same. We find ourselves constantly in the presence of writings that invite us into the joy of words, into a well-shaped language, in a form that demands from us the attention that we give to poetry and awakens us to expectation.

2.

Certain scholars of the Bible have long known that biblical poetry is not there simply to add a dash of nobility, or sublimity, or emotive force to what the author could have said in prose. They learned from literary critics what the critics had learned from poets: poetry is in itself a way of thinking and of imagining the world; it discovers with precision what it had to say only by saying it; the meaning of a poem awaits us in its manner of being, and meaning in the customary sense of the word is not what is most important about it. Being attentive to biblical poetry as such does not lead to a purely literary appreciation of the text, but rather to a vigorous effort to understand it as it wants to be understood, so as to receive it and assimilate it as it is.

And yet, the question remains: Why is there so much poetry in the Bible? The answer is unproblematic if one takes the Bible to be a library of purely human books, of remarkable interest but grounded in outdated beliefs. In that case the presence of poetry is accounted for by the poetic gift of its authors. But if one considers the Bible to be the revelation of a God (whatever the modalities of that revelation), and if one allows that the biblical authors were inspired (in one way or another) to write in this way, why did they, in a sense, complicate their task by devoting so much care and exactitude to the form of their writings, and so leave us "meanings" or "messages" to be sought in the very movements of their language?

Beyond the study of the structures of Hebrew poetry and of the range of poems that these structures underlie, should we not ask ourselves if the presence of so many poems changes not only the way in which the Bible speaks to us, but also the kind of message, or announcement, or call that it conveys? How must faith perceive biblical speech? What does this continual turn to poetry imply about the very nature of Christianity?

We can start to respond to these questions by giving some thought to how we usually read poetry. We do not paraphrase poems, extracting a meaning and leaving aside the redundant form. It is the very being itself of the poem that matters, the sounds and the rhythms that animate it like a living thing, the relations that the words stitch among themselves through their memory and their history, and the connotations that they disseminate. This in no way presupposes reading in a "poetic state" excluding reason, as Henri Bremond proposed in *Prière et poésie* (1926). Commenting on the difference between the famous opening line of Keats's *Endymion*: "A thing of beauty is a joy for ever," and the line that Keats first wrote: "A thing of beauty is a constant joy," Bremond rightly judges that it is only in the final version that "the current flows." But he affirms at the same time that between "a constant joy" and "a joy for ever," "the intellectual nuance, if there is such a nuance, is infinitely small." On the contrary, it is immense! A beauty that constitutes "a constant joy" remains in the memory and accompanies us in life. From this perfectly true but banal thought, Keats, in revising the line and no doubt through one of those unforeseen and inexplicable leaps that have led us to invent the Muse, draws a far greater and properly poetic thought. "A joy for ever" means what it says, the meaning is in the words themselves: a natural beauty or the beauty of an imaginary story brings us joy in that it reveals what transcends life; to see beauty is to glimpse a sort of eternity. Just as the ear catches the enthusiastic rhythm of the line's ending, with the accent that falls on *joy* and the words *for ever* that impose and seem to prolong themselves thanks to the extra eleventh syllable, the intelligence, while also *listening*, catches the wonderful idea that took form.

However, while we read a poem of Keats, or of Baudelaire or Ronsard, in this way, we easily forget our customary attention to the life of the poetic word when reading, for example, a psalm, from which we want to draw a teaching, a lesson. We need to be reminded of two well-known *pensées* of Pascal: "Different arrangements of words make different meanings, and different arrangements of meanings produce different effects"; "The same meaning changes according to the words expressing it."[1] Indeed, the meaning *changes*, and not only in poetry: Pascal speaks here of prose. The second fragment continues: "Meanings are given dignity by words instead of conferring it upon them." I know no better formula for suggesting the inseparability of words and meanings. And if it is important not to depart from a biblical text written in prose, all the more so should we remain as close as possible to a biblical poem, knowing that poetry, which does not permit paraphrase, also does not convey propositions—or conveys them in a context that gives them their specificity. It seems to me that we do not have to draw doctrines from the Bible other than those that the biblical writers themselves found there, for we cannot touch bottom in these deep waters; the world that is revealed to us entirely exceeds us. We can understand only what God reveals to us. The intelligence that he has given us allows us to reflect on what we read, but any attempt to go further, and above all systematic theology— whether it results in the *Summa Theologiae* of Thomas Aquinas or the *Institutes of the Christian Religion* of Calvin—seems an error.

To believe in the Bible—or rather, to believe the Bible, and allow oneself to be convinced that it is the word of God, in whatever way one considers it—is to believe what it says, with a supernatural faith that resembles, at an infinite distance, the confidence with which we read a poem, accepting that its reality is found in it and not in our exegeses. This allows for adhering to the truth that is at once included in the words and liberated by them, whatever the difficulty posed by the Flood, for example, or the Tower of Babel. We do not necessarily know the exact nature of the truth that is revealed to us, but we know where to look for it, just as we do not necessarily understand a poem, but we look for the answer to our questions in the poem itself, without adding or subtracting anything.

3.

Poetry attracts our attention to language and to the mystery of words, to their capacity to create, almost by themselves, networks of meaning, unexpected emotions, rhythms and a music for the ear and for the mouth that spreads through the entire body and all one's being. It acts similarly on the world, by finding for the presences of the real new names, and associations of words, of cadences, of sounds, that give to the most familiar beings and objects a certain strangeness that is both disturbing and joyous. It burns up appearances, it uncovers the invisible, it opens, like a little casement or a great window, onto the unknown, onto *something else*. The shade of trees that invites us in the midst of strong heat is transfigured when Racine's *Phèdre* cries:

> *Dieux! que ne suis-je assise à l'ombre des forêts!*
> [Gods! why am I not seated in the shade of forests!]

Reason or good sense might object that one cannot be seated in the shade "of forests," but only in the shade of a tree, or if one pictures it in the mind, in the shade of a forest, in the singular. These plural forests constitute a world seen anew, re-created by the imagination, a world of great beauty that is almost cerebral, but that at the same time in no way loses contact with reality. We are attracted, like Phèdre in speaking, by the grave sonority of "*ombre*," which contrasts with the *i* sounds that precede it: "*que ne suis-je assise . . .*" The coolness of this shade, under forests that have become protecting and enveloping, creates for Phèdre an eminently desirable place, apt to save her from her burning unavowable love for Hippolyte and from the terrible gaze of the gods. The beneficial shadow trembles with a devastating passion; the imagined place is filled with human guilt.

The "meaning" of the famous verse depends on the imagination that inhabits it, and on the emotion that animates it, which would not be fully present without its grammar and without the sounds that it makes. The forests, real, surreal, and resonating with the character's desire, shame, and aspiration, represent, in a sudden vision, the true world: loved, lost, possible. And I do not exclude the likelihood that these "*forêts*" are imposed on Racine by the necessity of rhyming them with "*apprêts*" at the end of the preceding line, and by the impossibility of writing the four syllables "*de la forêt*." The arrival of poetry for a prosaic reason is not at all shocking: essential words and ideas frequently arrive in an oblique manner.

As Henri Bremond writes, poetry produces in us "a feeling of presence." The world is *there*, not under its usual guise, but in a language that alone can give it immediacy. The poetic act draws close to the real and, in order to go to the depth of things, it re-creates them for us by welcoming them in sounds, rhythms, and unlimited ramifications of meanings, and places these re-creations in the domain of the possible. In its own way, and without at all being supernatural, poetry too is a revelation. The Bible as revelation and as poetic speech gives equally and above all onto *something else*. Clearly, it does not develop exclusively in poems, but its writings often turn into verse, as if it tended toward poetry, by supposing poetry to be the speech most appropriate to the strangeness, to the transcendence of what it manifests. And let us think again of the words of Jesus. He speaks quite often in parables, in order to present complex truths in the form of stories and within the life of a few characters, and in order to provoke his listeners—and us, his readers—to search, each time, for meaning in the multiple facets of a fiction. His affirmations in prose are equally poetic in that they are not understood right away; they ask that we receive them as we receive poetry, by becoming conscious of the mystery that accompanies them. For example, in hearing "the kingdom of heaven is very near," or "this is my body," or "I am the truth," we feel, I believe, something other than propositions, and we recognize behind these very simple words a sort of hinterland of meaning that we must explore as one explores the depths of a poem.

"I am the truth" escapes from all the modes of thinking in Western philosophy.

Jesus, who is the Word, *speaks*, indeed, and does not write. Everything he says follows from a particular situation, from a lived moment. And so many books of the Bible began by being said, or were destined, like the Psalms, to be said and sung; or gathered the words of an orator, like Ecclesiastes, or presuppose a dialogue, like Job or the Song of Songs. The Bible engages us constantly in listening, in becoming sensitive to the ways of writing, to images that do not explain and, ideally, to the music of thought. It is true that most of us do not have access to the original texts, but wasn't that foreseen? There are ways to understand, even at a distance, how Hebrew and Greek function, and it is up to us to seek in a simple translation, on the condition that it is poetically faithful, the animation of the speech and the way and the life of the truth.

Reading the Bible is a "poetic" experience. It offers us a theology according only to the etymological sense of the word: speech concerning God. For the Bible, which puts us in front of *something else*, is itself other. Have we, in Europe, truly grasped the nature of Christianity? Haven't we instead assimilated to our categories of thought and our habits of reading a religion that comes to us from the Middle East? Its Jewish origins in no way signify that Christianity lacks a universal bearing, but they must not be neglected. God chose to reveal himself first through a people that had, century after century, their own way of thinking and writing, and the religion they transmitted bears the marks of this genesis. The Bible asks us to recognize the strangeness, the *foreignness* of Christianity, and to put into question our European manner of approaching it. Recovering this Christianity that comes from elsewhere would change our reading of the Bible, and doubtless our way of proclaiming the Gospel.

What I am proposing has nothing to do with the tendency, in a civilization referred to as post-Christian, to present the Bible as a literary treasure, a work offered for the reader's admiration whose strength and authority would lie in the genius of its authors. Nor am I trying to promote a great poetic vision of Christianity that would sweep aside anything in the Bible that might bother us, such as sin, redemption, or the resurrection. That would be as badly inspired as the movement in the nineteenth century to replace Jesus as Son of God and Presence in the life of his believers with Jesus the great moral exemplar who, stripped of all his works and merely human, is not going to meddle in our affairs. A poetic reading of the Bible implies neither an abdication of reason (but it is necessary to know how and where to reason), nor a sort of literary quietism in which one would be absorbed in the meditation on texts to the point of neglecting to live in conformity with what they say. A poetic reading of the Bible is simply an invitation to rediscover Christianity, right there where it is to be found, and as it presents itself.

A FEELING OF PRESENCE

I.

THE OTHERNESS of Christianity became clear to me the very moment I became a Christian. I speak of this conversion because of my conviction that every truth passes through an individual and thus takes on a particular color, and because everything, or almost everything, that I will have to say in this book flows from this strange experience. I even ask myself whether everything that has been given to me to think since then, regarding the Bible, literature, painting, music, or philosophy, does not originate there. My conversion proves nothing, but I do not offer it as a proof.

As a child and an adolescent in long-ago England, I had the good luck, not being a Christian, of being more or less completely unaware of Christian doctrines. With no one in my family interested in religion, the subject was never brought up. It is true that the instruction in primary and then in "grammar school" was not constrained by French laicity, and, according to tradition, we assembled every morning in the great hall for the "assembly," where we sang a hymn and listened to the headmaster read the "collect for the day" from the Anglican liturgy before we all mumbled the Lord's Prayer together. We were not expected to understand, and from this point of view I was a model student. Among the disciplines taught in the small classes was "Scripture," but this essentially consisted of learning about the apparently interminable missionary journeys of Saint Paul. I also remember that on certain evenings in December I would go with friends to sing Christmas carols at people's front doors, in the hope of receiving a few pence, and that my mother taught me, when I was very small, some children's hymns. So what pushed me, at the age of nineteen, to become interested in Christianity?

During the summer of 1957, before going up to Cambridge University, I was fascinated and at the same time deeply troubled by the simple intuition that another way of knowing existed, one beyond reason and the senses. I felt imprisoned by a traditional and humanist epistemology, one in no way unique to that era, that had been transmitted to me by the sort of teaching that was developed in the English grammar schools from their creation in the sixteenth century, a teaching that made of the student an intelligence within a body, an individual apt to perceive the reality of the world and his own reality by using the resources of his brain and his sensations. Perhaps the poetry that had been living in me for many years—the poetry of others that I devoured, as well as my own, still feeble but of capital importance for me—had already revealed to me another world to know, and the necessity of another way, of another faculty, for discovering it. The questions that adolescents typically ask themselves: Who am I?, and above all, Am I? (an apparently absurd question, but which translates a radical sudden consciousness of the Fall), also put me on the right path, by prompting me to study how we know ourselves.

This sense of another dimension within the real, and of another cognitive capacity that it was urgently necessary to find within oneself, pushed me to reflect day after day, and to read whatever might help me. Of the books I read, William James's *The Varieties of Religious Experience*, published in 1902, enlightened me the most. It deals abundantly with conversions, mystical experiences, presentiments of a supernatural world, all of which was enough to rattle, by virtue of its strangeness, a young man shut in by the opposite presuppositions, whose arbitrariness he was already feeling. I doubtless latched on to certain of James's affirmations: "Mystical states . . . open out the possibility of other orders of truth," or, "Our normal waking consciousness, rational consciousness, as we call it, is but one special type of consciousness, whilst all about it, parted from it by the filmiest screens, there lie potential forms of consciousness entirely different." I also noted the absolute distinction that he drew, within the religious domain, between "belief that formulas are true" and "personal experience."[1]

I see now the limits of this great book, which studies the psychology and the philosophy of religious experience from the outside, assumes that there exist people "temperamentally qualified for faith," and seems to conceive of faith as a force within the individual rather than an engagement toward God.[2] Nevertheless, the insufficiency of everything I was reading, like that of everything everyone was telling me at the time, played a paradoxically essential role in my conversion. Everything can serve, and the weakness of human help underscores the necessity of having recourse to something else.

The quest upon which I had embarked was not merely a philosophical search. I felt above all that if I wanted to understand I needed to be in a different way, to open myself to that within the real that went completely beyond my capacity to know it. I felt that Christians had made the leap (I also was reading Kierkegaard), and that it was necessary to search in that area. One evening, walking in town, I stopped to listen to a speaker who, perched atop a makeshift platform and surrounded by some friends, was speaking about Christianity. The phenomenon was not rare: the habit of addressing the crowd on a chosen subject, most often political or religious, had been long established in the country, especially in Hyde Park, in London, where I had already listened to enthusiasts of many kinds. I later learned that this way of preaching the Gospel, which may seem weird and even irregular, goes back to the origins of Christianity and characterized the actions of John the Baptist or Saint Paul, as well as Jesus. After he was done I spoke to the preacher, a member of a Baptist church; he gave me a Bible; we struck up a friendship. In the weeks that followed I read the Bible, especially the New Testament, with an attention both feverish and perplexed, all the while noticing that I was not understanding very much. I posed a whole series of probably sterile questions to my friend as well as to another member of his church, to which, happily, they did not know how to respond. It was their way of living and their conviction that attracted me. I could have grasped the entire teaching of the New Testament through my intelligence without being any further along, while the living example of faith spoke to me at another level, and deepened my lack of satisfaction.

What did I retain from the Bible? First, that its discourse was like no other, that it had an authority that I had never come across before, even in Shakespeare, and that its word, so different, seemed addressed to me. Second, that what Jesus said of himself and what others said of him was probably exact, for a reason that I could not explain. I noticed little by little, despite the confusion of my mind and despite the very basic and erroneous vision that I had of the New Testament, that Christianity was the truth. My intuition, There is *something else*, became: There is an Other. I was conscious in only a vague way of sin and the need for salvation; the feeling of guilt came later. I knew only that I was not like I should be, and that I had to change completely.

This ignorance is instructive: we do not need to understand much in order to become Christian. We do not necessarily pass through the classic stages: conviction of sin, repentance, act of faith.

However, I found myself in front of a wall. I believed, or I believed that I believed, not because the Bible had convinced me by arguments, or by proofs (the Bible doesn't prove anything), but thanks to the strength of its word, which I now call poetic. And yet, if I understood one thing perfectly, it was that the belief that I had was good for nothing. No one asked me to believe in the existence of God the way I believed in that of China; no one wanted me to accept the death and the resurrection of Jesus as I could have accepted abstract expressionism or the market economy. It was clear to me that the fact of believing in what the Bible said, without any hesitation, didn't help me, and that giving myself entirely to this truth and to the very Source of the true changed nothing. What I needed in order to make a step forward was what I was looking for from the beginning, a different way of knowing, which I was powerless to bring about myself.

I suffered much from this need, until the day when I fell upon the healing of the epileptic demoniac as it is told in the Gospel of Mark

(9:14–29). After the Transfiguration, Jesus comes back down into the world of evil and unhappiness, where a father begs him to help his son whom a spirit torments, often casting him into the fire or into the water. Jesus replies: "If you can believe, everything is possible to him who believes." I understood right away that this word was addressed to me—"if you *can* believe"—and the response fell like a flash of lightning: *"Lord, I believe; help thou mine unbelief."* I quote the words that I read in the English Bible of 1611, the "authorized version" of King James. Like the father, I believed, but I knew already that God was demanding of me instead of this assent a faith entirely other and above my means, and that I was excluded from it. In an unforgettable instant, the father spoke for me, and Jesus responded to me, without words, but present in the room, that he was helping me, that he was giving me right then and there, with a big smile, the faith that he alone possessed. I melted in tears of joy.

I had not accomplished the leap of faith on my own. All the effort that I had made, and that continued in this tensed reading of the text, was transformed into a simple cry, which came from another as if from the depths of my being, and it was Jesus who strode across eternity to come to me.

2.

The written word became a voice once again at the moment I heard it. And it was the words themselves that accomplished their work, while so many modern translations fail to do so. In reading the Jerusalem Bible, "I do have faith! Help the little faith I have!" we understand that the translator wanted to *explain* the text, by proposing a reasonable interpretation: I have faith, but my faith is not complete. In the same spirit, the Bible du Semeur offers: "I believe, but help me, for I lack faith!" and the New English Bible: "I have faith … help me where faith falls short." Even certain marginal references added recently to the English Bible of 1611 seem to offer the same exegesis. But what does the Greek say? *"Pisteuō [kurie] boēthei mou tē apistia."*

The perfectly audible play between *pisteuō* and *apistia* is astonishing, because with this privative and contradictory *a-* the phrase seems like an oxymoron, saying in sum: "I believe and do not believe, I have faith and am without faith." The Vulgate translates it like this: "*credo adiuva incredulitatem meam*," thus preserving the simple and strong echo between the two opposing words. The translation published by English Catholics at Rheims in 1582, like the New Testament of the Port-Royal Bible of 1667, follows the Vulgate: "I do believe Lord: help my incredulity." All the time-honored English translators, from Wycliffe in the 1380s to the translators of 1611, saw that in order to translate what we hear in the Greek, they could profit from the even more striking passage from "believe" to "unbelief." Where did this later desire to rationalize come from? Why do we no longer listen to the Bible's very words, allowing their strangeness to teach us, to move us outside our reassuring habits of thinking? Do we not see all that we are losing?

For doesn't this absolute distinction between two kinds of faith create a new category of being? A category not found, for example, in Pascal, for whom "there are only three sorts of people: those who have found God and serve him; those who are busy seeking him and have not found him; those who live without either seeking or finding him."[3] Those who seek God without having found him and who are the readers Pascal would be addressing in the book of apologetics he was preparing, return in fragment L. 427: "I can feel nothing but compassion for those who sincerely lament their doubt, who regard it as the ultimate misfortune, and who, sparing no effort to escape from it, make their search their principal and most serious business."[4] Pascal is certainly right to consider that between the Christians and the atheists there are those who doubt, but according to the biblical verse that my experience verified, there also exist those who do not doubt, who believe, but who at the same time are deprived of true faith. All of Pascal's effort aims at helping the people who do not believe, and who, like his interlocutor in fragment L. 418, would be able to cry out, "I am so made that I cannot believe." The remedy, since the "powerlessness to believe" comes in this case from the passions, despite the fact that "reason" leads to believing, is to diminish the passions, since the passage between unbelief and belief would be opened, according to other fragments, thanks to "proofs." But for the feeling of desolation and urgency that I knew between faith and faith, passions and proofs are beside the point.

One continues to grasp the importance of words in looking closer, throughout this passage, at Mark's precise and felicitously repetitive writing. In imploring Jesus to help (*boēthei*) his unbelief, the father reiterates in a new context the prayer that he already addressed to Jesus regarding his son: "Come to our aid" (*boēthēson*). The word is deepened, the need is felt now in the inner life of the individual. When the spirit sees Jesus, it "immediately" (*euthys*) convulses the child; when the father understands the challenge that Jesus throws him ("If you can believe"), which is what is at stake and at the same time his own true condition, he "immediately" (*euthys*) begs Jesus to rescue him. The word is deepened anew at this second, decisive moment of realization of the person of the Lord. When Jesus learns that his disciples were unable to expel the spirit, he complains of this "unbelieving" (*apistos*) generation; in admitting his own "unbelief" (*apistia*), the father once again deepens the word further, recognizing an absence that exists at an entirely different level. Each time, the language is repeated not in a mechanical fashion, but in order to probe more deeply into the father's experience. What a shame to dissipate all of this in the translation by failing to notice this illuminating rhetoric! I also regret the recent tendency to translate in a different way the crucial sentence of Jesus that elicits the father's reaction. The father, having said to Jesus, "If you can do anything [*et ti dunasai*], come to our aid," is met with a reply from Jesus that, according to the old translations, puts the father in front of his own responsibility: "If you can believe [*ei dunasai pisteusai*], all is possible for him who believes." The choice of a different lesson (a different translation of the Greek words from Mark 9:23, *ei dunē*) gives rise to a less striking verse: "'If you can!' said Jesus. Everything is possible for him who believes." In the old translations, including the Vulgate, Jesus turns back on the father the words that he said—if *you* can, if you can *believe*—and it is to this that the father reacts, from the depths of his soul.

I see now (I was not sensitive to this at the time) that in the English translation all the words of the father's response come from the language's Germanic stock: "Lord, I believe; help thou mine unbelief." As is often the case with other writers, and in a particularly moving way in Shakespeare, a cry that comes from the heart of the soul finds words to articulate itself in the ancient roots of the language, the ones that are buried deep in the very being of the English. The words also compose a verse, in iambic pentameter. The charm, the magical song of the phrase that immediately penetrated my awareness, illuminating a threshold and bringing me across it, arose without any doubt from this poetic concentration of the language.

3.

The coexistence of belief and an absence of belief, with the uncomfortable feeling of finding oneself between the two, constitutes an important element of spiritual psychology. Curiously, it is scarcely mentioned. And this way of becoming Christian taught me many things. First, that it is impossible for us to believe in God. Adam did not need to do so in the perfection of the first world, since he knew God and heard his voice. In the world to come we will not need to do so either, for, as the apostle Paul says, we see now "in a mirror, in an enigma, but then face to face," and if, presently, "I know in a partial way . . . then I shall know as I am known" (1 Corinthians 13:12). In the interval of the fallen world, however, the belief we are capable of is not the faith that saves. Even this first belief, which we seem to gain by our own efforts, probably comes to us from the grace of God; the true faith is quite evidently out of our reach—for our own good, so that we recognize that we depend, as creatures and above all as sinners, on the goodness of the Creator and the Savior. In a sense, it is frustrating: all this seeking, all this intense concentration, all this anguish and all this hope, only to wind up at a dead end—except the dead end is the preeminently salutary place.

This seems obvious once we admit that faith is a gift of God. But there is an abyss between learning, through religious instruction or through reading the New Testament, that believing in God is an effect of grace, and being convinced of it by experience, by the disagreeable fact of finding oneself excluded from an infinitely attractive universe, before being admitted to it through the benevolence of an Other. And this presence of the gift has certainly nourished my reflection in other areas, particularly that of poetry, where what is essential in the poetic act seems to me to come from elsewhere (without there being a question of supernatural inspiration), and in the area of thinking, where each idea comes at a precise point with a suddenness that never fails to astonish me. When I succeed in understanding something after much effort, I always have the impression that it was *given* to me to understand.

The discovery of a chasm between the faith that I could bring about and the authentic faith that was escaping me also had the consequence of making evident to me the otherness of Christianity. *Something else* existed in the real; the Christian religion did not present itself as a systematic explanation of reality, to be approved of or rejected; in order to reach it I needed a way of knowing that I did not possess. Or, as Pascal says with admirable concision (in another context, it is true): "Christianity is strange."[5] The father's very formula— "I believe; help thou mine unbelief"—affected me like poetry, with this oxymoronic and mysterious play between the positive and the negative. I understood later why: poetry is also strange, for it likewise has the task of allowing a glimpse of what transcends us.

I also discovered in the weeks that followed the radical nature of the new world that was appearing, and of the new self that it was necessary to become in order to see it. Regarding the self, I fell upon some prodigious verses. Christians, says the apostle Peter, are "born anew, not of corruptible seed but of incorruptible: the living and eternal Word of God" (1 Peter 1:23). These same Christians, says the

Gospel of John, are "children of God" and "were born not of blood nor of the will of the flesh nor of the will of man, but of God" (John 1:13). This new spiritual birth demands resources that we do not have, since it exceeds our *corruption* and our *will*. It recalls, all proportions maintained, the birth of Jesus and, behind it, the entire series of prominent and miraculous births in the Bible in which women who are too old or sterile become, despite everything, despite sin and the inert weight of a fallen world, the mothers of Isaac, of Joseph, of Samson, of Samuel, and of John the Baptist. To become Christian, as I learned very early, is not to change one's opinion, to adhere to dogmas, to opt for a different way of considering reality, but to be born anew—*to be* new; to become an other in a world that is also transfigured. For it is the entirety of our experience, everything that appears to us under the sign of interiority and exteriority (but these are imperfect categories) that undergoes a profound change. The apostle Paul perfectly grasps the simultaneity of an other self and an other world when in his second letter to the Corinthians he affirms *"ei tis en christō, kainē ktisis"* (5:17). This is translated: "For anyone who is in Christ, there is a new creation" (Jerusalem Bible), or "Thus, the one who is united to Christ is a new creation" (Bible du Semeur), or "When anyone is united to Christ, there is a new world" (New English Bible). In every case the choice (as was already so in the Vulgate and in the English translation of 1611) is between two possible meanings: the self is changed or the world is changed, while the Greek says, quite simply and by opening wide the doors of meaning: "If someone is in Christ, new creation." The idea is immense: in relation to the first Creation, of the heavens and the earth, a new creation takes place with each conversion. It allows the new creature that is the Christian to catch a glimpse, in and around him- or herself, of a new universe. What happens to him and what happens to his world, or to his way of seeing this world, anticipates, here and now, the second Creation at the end of time, when God will conceive a "new heavens" and a "new earth" (2 Peter 3:13, and elsewhere). The sentence's form is once again poetic. The absence of a verb and a referent, which would limit the meaning, allows for naming, directly and mysteriously, the new phenomenon, the sudden appearance everywhere of the unforeseeable.

And that is the other thing I learned, and of which I already spoke: the words themselves of the Bible vibrate with power, and refraining from muzzling this power must be the translator's first concern. Earlier I brought up the desire to explain texts through paraphrase, as if the translator had no confidence in the text itself and found it necessary to help it express itself and touch the reader. As if the translator didn't realize that if the author had wanted to write, for example, "Come in aid to my little faith," he would have done so. The exegete always runs the risk of putting himself in the place of the translator, he who should listen to the text and seek to grasp how it works. In his letter to the Ephesians, Paul urges them to behave as wise beings, "redeeming the time, because the days are evil" (5:16). The Vulgate, the English Bible of 1611, the Port-Royal Bible, and up to the Bible Segond in its 1962 revision translate this passage by trusting the apostle, and not their own interpretation. The stake is considerable: it seems that the Christian must "redeem" the time just as Christ "redeemed" us from the curse of the law (Galatians 3:13), and it is true that we struggle to grasp how that can be. But Paul uses the same expression in the letter to the Colossians (4:5), and we do not have to dilute his thought by having him tell the wise "to make the best use of your time" (Jerusalem Bible), or "Profit from the opportunities that present themselves to you" (Bible du Semeur), or "Use the present opportunity to the full" (New English Bible). One of the possible meanings of the purposefully mysterious words is extracted, losing in the process the whole dimension of the text that makes us reflect and invites us, as poetry does, to travel beyond the known. A note in the Bible de Jérusalem informs the reader that the Greek means literally, "Who redeem the time." Indeed, and the Greek is right!

Expressions full of imagery can be especially tempting for the translator, prompting him to come to the readers' aid. When Ecclesiastes counsels, "Cast your bread upon the waters, after a long time you will find it again" (11:1), the gesture captures the attention, just as the bread on the water, which goes away and comes back, grounds the reflection in a concrete image. The Jerusalem Bible and the Bible du Semeur, like the old translations, retain the image, but the translators of the New English Bible orient the reader toward a positive and rational action: "Send your grain across the seas, and in time you will get a return." The prize for the most prosaic and the most self-seeking translation goes to the Good News Bible, a popular American translation: "Invest your money in foreign trade, and one of these days you will make a profit." The poetry disappears completely, and with the poetry goes the feeling of *something else*, an opening onto the unknown.

DRAW ME A GOD

I.

TRANSLATORS sometimes permit themselves to make small modifications of the text of the Bible by interpreting it. Theologians change it even more when they follow, in part unwittingly, the pathways of European thought. For the latter and the former, their motives are pure, their consciences at peace, but they nevertheless give in to a temptation. It is to be feared that in this context and in certain circumstances, paraphrase is diabolical speech.

The devil's trick consists in substituting for the word of God another word, contrary and equivocal, such as that of the serpent in Genesis ("You will not die" [3:4]), or most generally a word that is approximate. This trick veils the divine language and aims to stifle its authority and power. I bring up this antiword with fear and trembling, understanding quite well that it is on the lookout for me in this book, without any doubt.

Theology is necessary, but theologians, our precious allies, should tell themselves over and over again that the Bible, a stranger to our habits, was not written for philosophers. The biblical logos has its own logic; we are in unknown territory. The book of Proverbs was composed and assembled, the introduction tells us, "to penetrate proverbs and obscure sayings, / the words of the wise and their riddles" (Proverbs 1:6). We could persuade ourselves that this *indirection* of the revealing word belongs to the genres of proverbs and prophecies, to the rhetorical conduct of the Old Testament, and perhaps to the literary genius of the Hebrew people. But what does Jesus say about the kingdom of heaven? He never says that it is defined in this way or that, by propositions to be dissected; he always says that it lets itself be glimpsed through comparisons to ponder, or in short stories that must be explored. The kingdom of heaven is like "a man sowing good seed in his field" (Matthew 13:24), like "a grain of mustard seed which a man took and sowed" (13:31), like "leaven which a woman took and hid in three measures of flour" (13:33), like "a treasure hidden in a field" (13:44) or "a merchant in search of fine pearls" (13:45) or "a net which was thrown into the sea" (13:47). It is like "a king who wished to settle accounts with his servants" (18:23), like "a householder who went out early in the morning" (20:1), like "a king who gave a marriage feast for his son" (22:2), like "ten virgins who took their lamps and went to meet the bridegroom" (25:1), like "a man who, going on a journey, called his servants" (25:14). Each time, we try to discern the kingdom of heaven thanks to comparisons that make us understand that it escapes our comprehension and that we can approach it only through imagination and lived experience. The numerous stories that Jesus tells do not belong merely to the parable genre: they indicate that the kingdom of heaven is indeed "near," that it fills the here and now and the fabric of life.

Yes, one might answer, but Jesus speaks in parables, or literary narratives, in "enigmas" to the crowd because the power of knowing "the mysteries of the kingdom of heaven" was not granted to them (Matthew 13:11); to his disciples he explains everything. And yet, he explains to them only the allegory that the parable contains: the man who sows the good seed, for example, is the Son of man, the field is the world, the good seed is the kingdom's subjects, and so on. What the kingdom of heaven is remains a mystery; we continue to have a premonition of it in an abundance of concrete situations, in the thickness of existence. And after all, these parables appear in the Bible—why did the evangelists not simply retain the explanations alone, when there are any? The parables are addressed to us, too, so that we read them poetically, according to the meaning I would like to give to this word. They do not stop accomplishing their work, between what is secret and what is transparent.

The kingdom of heaven is *like*... For us, there is the figurative, the image (Genesis 1:26); for God alone there is the thing itself.

Interpretation is indispensable and it is true that as such it does not originate in European traditions. In the Jewish tradition glosses and glosses of glosses of the Hebrew Bible were already accumulating. However, intellectual passion in the West aspires, with a movement beyond simple exegesis, to attain a totalizing vision, to build a universal architecture for the mind. Claudel's enthusiasm (in his "Discours de réception à l'Académie française") for one particular attempt, singularly impressive and marvelously ordered, is understandable: "Saint Thomas on the foundations of revelation builds with the syllogism his immense edifice."[1] (In a few words one hears the strength of Claudelian syntax and rhythm.) But this is the problem. Thomas Aquinas *works* on the foundations of the Bible in order to construct his own work—the theological philosophy of Saint Thomas—which can appear, in its minutely close-fitting order, more coherent and even larger than the Bible. And what is the syllogism doing here, a form of reasoning unknown to the biblical authors? I remember, in my readings before my conversion, what Kierkegaard said in his journals about the most admirable recent effort to contain the world in thought: that if Hegel had seen in his system a mere intellectual experiment, one would say he was the strongest of all thinkers. In their self-sufficiency such systems of thought move away from life, where the individual is in question, with his choices to make and his duty to think not only with the mind, but with everything that constitutes the person.

One draws a European philosophy from the biblical word by making *theology for theology's sake*, just as *art for art's sake* was practiced in the nineteenth century, and in doing so one runs the same risk: that of making an idol of one's discipline. One answers questions that the Bible does not formulate. The writers of the New Testament are totally indifferent, for example, to the "problem" posed by the fact that Jesus was without sin yet at the same time born of a woman. No one denies, moreover, this indifference. And it is very difficult for us not to denature the biblical word with our ways of thinking and our vocabulary. The temptation remains alive to imitate the school of Alexandria, which wanted to show the compatibility between biblical revelation and Greek philosophy in order to recommend Christianity to educated people. Even if we know to avoid this trap (the biblical message comes from elsewhere; it teaches the truth to a sinful humanity; it has no need to prove its credentials), we fall into another. We say that God is "pure essence" or "pure transcendence," or that Jesus is "consubstantial" with the Father. We distinguish habitual grace from actual grace, sufficient grace from efficacious grace, as if we could break down God's eternal solicitude toward us. Through dissatisfaction with the Bible's ways of talking and its refusal to elucidate everything, we lose our way.

2.

How do we talk about God? In order to do it, certain passages of the Bible use negative adjectives, evoking the "uncorruptible" (Romans 1:23) or "invisible" (Colossians 1:15) God, and seem to support the partisans of "negative theology." Do these passages not strengthen the thesis that argues that, because God is beyond the reach of our categories, we can affirm not what he is, but only what he is not? It is nevertheless regrettable to transform this perception of the strangeness of God into a system, by forgetting that the God of the Bible, who loves us, in no way resembles the source of this theology—the One of Plato's *Parmenides*, unknowable and ineffable. Indeed, we fail to recall that it is not up to us to decide what language is appropriate for speaking of a God who revealed himself. The Bible affirms, through the mouth of Jesus, that God is "good" (Luke 18:19), and that God "is true" (John 3:33), and we note that John uses, without the least worry in the world, the verb *to be*. It is up to us to reflect on these affirmations, while pondering how the goodness, the truth, and the being of God stand infinitely far from our poor conceptions. In the revelation that "God is love" (1 John 4:16), we grasp that in God love and being merge, and that our task is existential rather than metaphysical: to try to live in such a way that on our level, too, being and loving come close and join together.

Other declarations are "poetic" and appeal to the imagination. For example: "God is light" (1 John 1:5). If we try to explain these few words by paraphrasing them, we lose their dazzling simplicity. Nearly everything the Bible says of God is simple—brief and jargon-free—as if to suggest that the incommensurable immensity of the Creator culminates (like certain equations that sum up a scientific conception of his universe) in a concentration of infinite power. Above all we lose the opportunity to probe this light, which, without being that of the sun, the stars, lightning, or fire, invites us to think of those presences, far away and near, as figures of the real light. We also lose the possibility of deepening at once both *God* and *light*, cutting short the study of the strange union that their placement in relation to each other supposes. When Stephen at the beginning of his speech before the Sanhedrin evokes "the God of glory" (Acts 7:2), he recalls numerous passages from the Old Testament that set forth in history this image of a splendor in God, of a singular shining forth that, as Keats wrote with regard to the silent form of a Greek urn and eternity, "teases us out of thought." Stephen also affirms that the glory of God "appeared" to Abraham; and upon ending his discourse, he himself, the text says, saw "the glory of God." This divine light's alterity is such that it does not preclude a ray adapted to our mind from ever reaching us. However, when Jesus says to the Samaritan woman that God is "spirit" (John 4:24), he seems to put an end to all discussion. By saying that he must be worshipped "in spirit" (4:23), Jesus encourages us to penetrate this extraordinary word, to approach God by searching for the manner of being that, miraculously, ties us to him. If we really must add something, the most useful thing would be to refer to the well-known fact that the Greek word for spirit, like the Hebrew word, means at the same time "spirit," "wind," and "breath": that which lifts us, surrounds us, and touches us with an invisible hand, inhabits us and makes us live.

Of all the "names" of God in the Bible, probably the one most fundamental for us is "the living God." It runs through the Old and

New Testaments. "My heart and flesh sing for joy / to the living God" (Psalms 84:2), and Paul carries it on: "We have set our hope on the living God" (1 Timothy 4:10). "The living God is among you," says Joshua to the Israelites (Joshua 3:10), and Peter replies to Jesus, standing in front of him: "You are the Christ, the Son of the living God" (Matthew 16:16). We seek the *life* of God, which moves among us, a life that is not ours but of which a living face, a living landscape, a living work, gives us a faint but eloquent sign.

How much more joyful are the biblical ways of speaking of God, compared with what theology can invent! The Bible is enough to convince us that God is marvelously other, infinitely beyond our intelligence, and that human language, in counting off his attributes, must not lead us to suppose that his justice, for instance, would be an oversize version of our own. As for God's being, which it is not appropriate to confuse with all the other beings that enter our experience, including ourselves: Does it not present itself to us precisely as a Life, which loves, which creates, which redeems, which judges, which draws near to and moves away from us? Instead of extracting an idea of God from the Bible, in regard to which one poses questions of theological philosophy by deploying a discourse that separates us from the "God of Abraham, of Isaac, and of Jacob" (as Pascal put it in the "Mémorial" of his late 1654 vision of the Lord), shouldn't we accept the ways of speaking of God that come to us from a civilization very different from our own? Shouldn't we nourish ourselves with each of these "names" of God, together if we can, but above all separately and in their biblical context, so as to encounter more and more intimately the Unnamable who condescended to be named?

"He who comes to God," says the letter to the Hebrews, "must believe that He is [*hoti esti*]" (Hebrews 11:6). If it seems curious to Europeans, to the sons of the Greeks, that the author does not stop to ponder the question of being, would it not be fitting to listen to him and to follow him, understanding that for him the being of God is first of all a life, a presence, a gift, or as he immediately puts it, that God "rewards those who seek him"? Even speaking of "the being" of God leads us away from the text, and from the God of the Jews and the first Christians, and shows the difficulty that we experience in staying close to the unfathomable biblical simplicity. Let us tell ourselves instead that God is Life, a loving presence ceaselessly at work in his creation, among his creatures, and let us apply ourselves to going deeper into, not ontology, but the at once clear and always mysterious declarations of God and of Jesus. For we know that for Moses God names himself "I am the one who is," or "I am; that is what I am" (Exodus 3:14), and that he continues with an even shorter formula, both clarifying and enigmatic: "You will say to the Israelites: 'I am' has sent me to you." What could we add, and why? Instead, let us try to dive into this "I am" who is the sole source of our derived being, into this Person before whom our persons are masks and figures. We likewise know that Jesus appropriates the (to a certain degree) effable name of God by responding to the incredulous Jews: "Before Abraham was born, I am [*egō eimi*]" (John 8:58). The Greek translation of his words avoids neither the verb *to be* nor the pronoun of subjectivity; the Son of God agrees to play with human language, despite its insufficiency. And just as he presents the kingdom of heaven through a series of comparisons, he presents himself through a series of metaphors, making the divine "I am" bloom in our world. The process is fully poetic. "I am the bread of life," he says (John 6:35), "I am the light of the world" (8:12), "I am the door of the sheep" (10:7), "I am the good shepherd" (10:11, 14), "I am the resurrection" (11:25), "I am the way, the truth, and the life" (14:6), "I am the true vine" (15:1). *Egō eimi*: each time, the most elementary, the shortest, and the most far-reaching divine name resonates within our reality, among our bread, our lights, our doors, our shepherds, our paths, our vines. It raises us above our worldly experience by revealing a spiritual meaning in familiar things and by inviting us at the same time to cherish the familiar opened to such dimensions. "I am the resurrection" takes up the belief in a resurrection on the last day in order to concentrate it on Jesus, who is the personification—what a strange idea!—of the resurrection, the truth, and the life.

We know that God's being is inaccessible to us, and we are eager to theorize its inaccessibility. Seeing clearly that it is beyond us, we want to enclose it in a philosophical system. Even the concept of the Trinity can lure us. An attempt to represent for ourselves with some clarity the forever mysterious relations among God the Father, the Son, and the Holy Spirit, it risks preventing us from entering more deeply, within their contexts, into the passages of the Bible where these names appear. It risks veiling what is *said*. As for knowing if God is the "pure act of being" (Thomas Aquinas), if his being precedes his goodness, if Jesus has two natures but one energy, if the Holy Spirit proceeds from the Father and from the Son or only from the Father, we need to realize that these inventions—and so many other inventions of philosophical theology, respectable in their way—answer questions that the Bible does not formulate, take us away from the only revelation, from the only truth that we have, and attest to the existence of a professional discipline that proceeds according to its own codes and constitutes a sui generis intellectual enterprise. (A similar problem is found in the domain of literary works, ever since literature entered the university as a discipline.) We can understand of God only what he has revealed to us; every attempt to go beyond that is, at base, ridiculous. And he has revealed so much to us! What else do we need? The effort to systematize revelation can be carried out only on our level and with our limited means. No set of human origin is capable of containing God, who alone knows the coherence of all things on earth and in heaven, and who gives us marvelous glimpses of it in the Bible. To try to grasp the Most High God, creator of the universe, from outside what he has delivered to us is to behave like a faithful dog, full of goodwill, who seeks to understand why his master especially appreciates the final quartets of Beethoven.

3.

The living God, indeed. Whence the error of another desire that constantly worries us: to prove the existence of God. But what is the condition, exactly, of those who do not believe in him? Unbelievers are first and foremost, as Paul says, "alienated from the life of God" (Ephesians 4:18). And what is an atheist, deep down? Paul's readers, converted pagans, were previously, he writes, "alienated from the community of Israel . . . having no hope and without God in the world" (Ephesians 2:12). "Without God," *atheoi*: the atheist is not merely the one who denies the existence of God by an act of his understanding and of his will that would leave him unscathed. He is every man, even the believer, who finds himself excluded, here and now, from the life of God. He is missing the true life, and access to its sole source. What he needs is not the certainty that an abstraction called "God" exists but the life of the living God. For God does not present himself as an object of thought to search for in the nowhere of the intelligence, but as a presence acting on the earth and everywhere, as Paul explains to the Ephesians: there is a God, he writes, a Father who is "above all and through all and in all" (Ephesians 4:6).

And yet, very early in the history of Christianity it was determined that it was good to demonstrate God's existence through reason, following the example of Plato and of Aristotle, without realizing that the difference between the Father of Jesus Christ and the Greek conception of God made every imitation problematic at the least. What is the true labor of reason for a Christian? It seems legitimate to want to gather together in a single vision the image of the world that faith gives, and thus to comprehend, under a Christian perspective, everything that composes our life, from anthropology and history to politics and all the forms of art. We work then within the space of speculation, where the ideas of today give way before the arguments of tomorrow, leaving behind in the best of cases a useful trace. It is clear that God engages us, too, in reflection on the links among the different parts of the biblical revelation, following the example of Paul, who, doubtless meditating on the speech of Stephen leading up to his martyrdom and rereading attentively the books that became the Old Testament, discerned precisely the relation between Moses and Abraham, between the Law and faith, and reaffirmed salvation by grace. The reading of his letters to the Galatians and to the Romans is a spiritual joy and at the same time an intellectual feast. The right use of reason brings joy to the mind, just as walking brings joy to the body.

We were given reason in order to exercise it within its proper domain, and determine its limits. It makes sense to know how far it is reasonable to reason, whether one is a believer or an unbeliever. The scientist who is convinced that his theories, experiments, and equations describe in a satisfying and complete fashion the phenomenal world that he studies without any need for the hypothesis of a "God" deludes himself in thinking that he has proved something, for the tools of his mind can discover only what they are adapted to detect. In order to catch sight of God in his creation he must have imagination and the gift of wonder; in order to see God there, he needs faith. One cannot prove either the existence or the nonexistence of God.

And what God are we talking about? It is enough to read the "proofs" of Anselm, Thomas Aquinas, Duns Scotus, Descartes, Leibniz, and Schelling, while having in mind verses 18–25 of the first chapter of Paul's letter to the Romans, which are supposed to be their foundation, to see the gulf that separates Paul, the precursor, from each of the successors. Hegel loses himself in the Idea of God, but he is not the only one to reduce God to a concept. At the endpoint of an argument that is always well constructed, skillful, fascinating, but in the end comical, there is nobody, there is only the word *God*, springing forth like a jack-in-the-box. When Descartes, in the fourth part of his *Discourse on Method*, argues that the "idea" of a being more perfect than him could not have come from him, and "so there remained only the possibility that the idea had been put into me by a nature truly more perfect than I was and even possessing in itself all the perfections of which I could have any idea, that is—to explain myself in one word—by God," one understands that philosophy in Europe made out of the idea of God, out of the word *God*, an idol.[2] We ourselves have decided what "God" is—as Descartes writes in the third of the *Meditations on First Philosophy*: "By the word 'God' I understand a substance that is infinite, eternal, immutable, independent, all-knowing, all-powerful"—and we have supposed, reck-lessly, that this God that we have invented corresponds to the God of the Bible.[3] The arguments that claim, with the best of intentions, to define God, to make him appear through the irresistible charm of words, prove as clearly as it is possible that whatever it pleases us to say about him, God escapes our thought.

Do we not hear the terrible irony in the letter of James? "You believe that God is one; you do well. Even the demons believe—and shudder" (James 2:19). Believing in the existence of God raises us to the level of the demons, who are not troubled by unbelief and doubt. With a few words, James sweeps away in advance the proofs of God by showing that the type of belief that they assume has nothing to do with faith. If starting tomorrow all men without exception, everywhere in the world, were to accept one or another of the proofs available, they would not be any more Christian than they are today. They would remain just as *atheist* as before, and the fact of having believed in a being of language would serve them ill, by turning them aside from seeking out who God is, and where to find him. The proofs of "God" lead us away from God, and from the manner in which the apostles announce him in Acts. Immediately after his conversion, Paul "pro-claimed Jesus" (Acts 9:20), the great Absentee from all proofs.

Even the expression, "I believe in God," which, coming from the Credo, seems obvious to us, can deceive us. Wouldn't it be better to say, as a fundamental proclamation of our faith, "I believe God"? Like Abraham, we believe a God who speaks to us. When God told the childless Abraham that he would nevertheless have a posterity as innumerable as the stars, Abraham "believed the Lord, and it was reckoned to him as righteousness" (Genesis 15:6). It is a capital mo-ment, since it grounds the justification by faith (Romans 4:3, Galatians 3:6), and by a faith that lives in its works (James 2:23), like that of Abraham at the moment when he readied himself to sacrifice his son after another word from God. In Greek, "to believe God," "to believe in God," and "to have trust in God" are said in the same way, and since God reveals himself, in Jesus, through the Bible, through cre-ation, and since he constantly communicates with us, it may be that the first of these expressions is at the heart of the others. God speaks to us and asks that we believe him.

4.

But this is not how theology presents him when, carried along by the impetus of its method, it aims likewise to demonstrate the truth of Christianity. The question is very much a present one. Pope Benedict XVI underscored the role of reason in the presentation of the faith. He called attention to Cardinal Newman, through his theological writings and then his journey to England for the beatification of Newman, whose influential book *An Essay in Aid of a Grammar of Assent* was published in 1870. Newman is such an attractive personality and such a great writer that I hesitate to criticize him. Nevertheless, this book, masterful in the accomplishment of the task the author assigned himself, highly interesting in terms of its composition, and completely right in certain of its orientations, represents a perspective on the approach to God, or believing God, that seems to me in the end mistaken.

The path he traces toward assent is much more persuasive and real than that of the old logical proofs, in which the signified "God" must exist because the order of reasoning necessitates it. Indeed, he writes, "I am not considering the question that there is a God, but rather what God is."[4] He is interested above all in the process of assent, for he also proposes "not . . . to set forth the arguments which issue in the belief of these doctrines" (God's Being, the Trinity), but "to investigate what it is to believe in them, what the mind does, what it contemplates, when it makes an act of faith." By pointing out that in numerous areas we accept propositions as true that we cannot prove, he tries to show that in the domain of faith, too, the convergence of several merely probable indices results not in a conditional acquiescence, but in an absolute certainty. And yet, always at issue here are propositions, even if Newman hastens to affirm that those that enunciate the Trinity, for example, express both "intellectual notions" and "things."[5]

In order to prepare his readers for the act of faith, he passes through "natural religion" and what "the system and the course of the world"[6] teach us, and through the testimony of the moral conscience, which, by teaching us good and evil, would allow us to truly apprehend "a Divine Sovereign and Judge."[7] He thus strives to create in his readers a certain "state of mind" necessary to "those who would inquire into the truth of Christianity."[8]

I am aware that in summarizing this book I veil its qualities and I leave in the shadows many surprising and felicitous ideas. Newman does not move among words and arguments but within the curiously disordered real. He looks into "this universal living scene of things" (268), and in order to determine the reciprocal relations between inference and assent, he advocates the study of "what the experience of human life, as it is daily brought before us, teaches us" (168). He treats his subject "not according to a priori fitness, but according to the facts of human nature, as they are found in the concrete action of life" (176). Regarding his theological research, he had already declared in his *Apologia Pro Vita Sua* (1864), "It was not logic that carried me on; as well might one say that the quicksilver in the barometer changes the weather. It is the concrete being that reasons; pass a number of years, and I find my mind in a new place; how? the whole man moves."[9] The abstract, he writes in the *Grammar*, "can only conduct to abstract."[10] In his polemic against Locke, the most famous of the English empiricists, who speaks of degrees of assent and who, enclosed for once in logic, believes that inference, necessarily conditional, can lead, despite the testimony of experience, only to an equally conditional assent, it is Newman who seems the more empirical of the two! Newman judges that Locke's conception of the human mind is "theoretical and unreal," and he criticizes him for having consulted "his own ideal of how the mind ought to act, instead of interrogating human nature, as an existing thing, as it is found in the world."[11]

Thus he moves away from a certain European way of thinking and recalls that Hebraic realism that I am trying to understand and promote. Nevertheless, his grammar of assent assumes that after a long process of reflection one is convinced of the truth of Christianity by an accumulation of proofs, which, if they are not of a purely logical and verbal order, lead in any case to the balanced acquiescence of an intellectual seated in his armchair; that is, to "one complex act both of inference and of assent."[12] Newman is speaking to those who are already moved by natural religion, and who have the sense of God and of sin, "which constitute the formal preparation for entering upon what are called the Evidences of Christianity."[13] The Evidences, which he enumerates at the end of the book, are traditional: the ability of Christianity alone to fulfill our aspirations, needs, and religious premonitions, the miracles, the fulfillment in the Messiah and in the Church of the promises of the Old Testament, the humanly inexplicable triumph of primitive Christianity, the endurance of the martyrs...It is possible that some come to Christianity in this way, having been troubled and then attracted by an apologetics of this sort. But is this faith—an encounter with a Person? (I know very well that the word *Person* is inadequate.) And doesn't faith come in a simpler and more rapid way, even for those who are used to complex and arduous reflection? It is probably revelatory that Newman quotes Mark 9:24 twice, giving it a meaning rather different from what I believed I discovered there during my conversion. Addressing the degree of strength or weakness that faith can have, he judges that the one who feels that his faith is feeble might say, along with the father of the demoniac, "I believe, help my unbelief!"[14] Farther on, he hears this cry as the expression of the "struggle between faith and unbelief."[15] I see there, and I dare to think that the father saw it as well, the petition of a man who believes with the energy that he finds within himself, but who sees that Jesus is asking him to believe in a different way, with the help of grace, the gift that he seeks to receive.

According to the Bible, it pleased God to give the faith that saves not through learned arguments, but through "the foolishness of preaching," through a message, centered on Christ crucified, which causes "scandal" (1 Corinthians 1:21, 23). We receive the good news of a religion revealed with the strength, indeed, of a revelation, of that which comes from elsewhere, through preaching, through listening to and reading the Bible, through biblical exegesis—an essential work of theologians, with the precise establishment of the texts. But Newman, believing that the Bible "is addressed far more to the imagination and affections than to the intellect,"[16] is persuaded that it needs propositions from theology in order to produce its full effect. There is nothing to object to when he states that several passages from the New Testament ring with the formula "The Son is God,"[17] and that numerous passages in the Old Testament draw their power, for Christians, from the related formula, "The Messiah is God."[18] The two propositions spring forth from the biblical texts. But what about the propositions that constitute the dogma of the Trinity, which he states in the following manner?

1. There are Three who give testimony in heaven, the Father, the Word or Son, and the Holy Spirit.
2. From the Father is, and ever has been, the Son.
3. From the Father and Son is, and ever has been, the Spirit.
4. The Father is the One Eternal Personal God.
5. The Son is the One Eternal Personal God.
6. The Spirit is the One Eternal Personal God.
7. The Father is not the Son.
8. The Son is not the Holy Ghost.
9. The Holy Ghost is not the Father.

For he says the following:

And if the New Testament be ... so real in its teaching, so lu-minous, so impressive, so constraining, so full of images, so sparing in mere notions, whence is this but because, in its references to the Object of our supreme worship, it is ever ring-ing the changes (so to say) on the nine propositions which I have set down, and on the particular statements into which they may be severally resolved?[19]

Newman comprehends quite well what sort of writing runs through the New Testament, and the Old, where all is real, full of images, and so removed from the conceptual, but *he doesn't hear it* that way. He assumes that, behind the texts as we read them, and serving to prop them up, there are "propositions" that in reality result from an ulterior theological labor. These propositions are uncertain; it is not to them that faith is given. He sees very well that "religion has to do with the real" and that "the real is the particular," but he adds that "theology has to do with what is notional, and the notional is the general and systematic. Hence theology has to do with the Dogma of the Holy Trinity as a whole made up of many propositions [that it regards] as a system of truth."[20] Theology goes beyond what biblical revelation teaches: with a "careful minuteness"[21] it "forms generalizations, and gives names to them," it "makes a survey and a catalogue of the doctrines" and "brings them together into a whole."[22] It proceeds according to what I call the European method; it has to do with the doctrines that result from revelation "through the exercise of abstraction and inference."[23]

5.

Why does Newman direct his apologetics toward assent to propositions and toward the convergence of proofs? Is it because he has his own adhesion to the Catholic Church constantly in mind, the long and laborious work that had convinced him to leave Anglicanism behind in order to find in Roman Catholicism the true tradition of the apostles? The essence of the *Grammar* is found in a paragraph in section III of his *Apologia Pro Vita Sua*, the book in which he explains his "conversion": he became Catholic through a "concatenation of argument."[24] In order to change churches an intellectual conviction is necessary, resulting from a study of texts and facts. After his turn to the Roman church (in 1845), he had at heart the desire to persuade his compatriots of the truth of Catholicism. Hence the terms of his letter to the wife of his friend William Froude: "The simple question you have to ask yourself is 'Have I a *conviction* that I *ought* to accept the Catholic Faith as God's Word?'"[25] Likewise the conclusion of a letter to Froude: "Let me add, that Catholics hold it would be wrong in any one becoming a Catholic without his *judgment* being convinced."[26] The memory of his studious passage not to Christian faith, which he had from the age of fifteen, but to another church, where his research had necessarily culminated in a decision grounded in the examination of probabilities and the exercise of judgment, seems to have colored his idea of true conversion.

True conversion, above all—and Newman knew this well—is the encounter with Christ. And what Christ teaches is himself. If one searches for the truth, he responds, "I am the truth." If one searches for the pathway to follow, the true life, and hope beyond death, he replies, "I am the path," "the life," "the resurrection." His glorious being is multiplied for us in a kaleidoscope of images: bread, the vine, the door, the shepherd . . . And faith in Christ is aroused by the Bible, received not as an invitation to philosophize, but as a "poetic" work. It is the very word of God, heard, preached, explained, that touches and disturbs. Have we lost the feeling of the power of this word by wanting to promote Christianity, by trying so hard to show it to be plausible and reasonable, or indeed, in certain settings and with a complete scorn for the biblical message, humanly attractive?

Invoking the power of the Bible does not amount to making it into an idol, since it is not the words that act, but the Spirit. Wordsworth spoke of the "presences of nature," having felt that the mountains, streams, and trees of the Lake District in England lived their own life, accompanied him in his walks, and opened his thought to the mysterious unity of the visible and the invisible. In the same spirit, Henri Bremond held, in a passage previously quoted, that poetry, even profane poetry, awakens "a feeling of presence," and allows us to draw near to the being of what it evokes. At a completely different level and if we are able to hear it, the Bible resounds with a divine Presence whose authority is in need of nothing to make itself felt.

THE LORD'S SUPPER

I.

WHICH leads us to the "Lord's supper," the privileged place where, just as the divine Presence makes itself felt, so too the words of the Bible, so simple, intelligible, and yet infinitely elevated above our intelligence, speak to us with the authority of Jesus and of the Holy Spirit. Here especially the word of God is sufficient: it tells the truth, asks to be heard, and resists paraphrase. Jesus's few remarks are truly "poetic": they lead us into the strange, into something else, into a mystery (in the current meaning of the word), and their strength condenses into their form.

This supper condemns in the most rigorous manner the quarrels among Christians. The act that should unite us—"For we being many," writes Saint Paul, "are one body: for we are partakers of that one bread" (1 Corinthians 10:17)—has brought about the most ill-tempered and bloody disputes. The situation is scandalous and deeply sad: we insult Jesus, who instituted this moment in part so that we should be in fraternal communion with one another. And I am persuaded that our divisions come from our incapacity to humbly accept what the Bible affirms, and to master the itch to gloss, to reason beyond what is revealed, to add human words to the word of God—to make clear, in sum, what the Holy Spirit has left obscure. It seems to me that a return to the very words that Jesus spoke during the Last Supper is necessary, and could bring us together. But I know very well that in this chapter where I am thinking only about reconciliation I will displease both Catholics and Orthodox, and disappoint Protestants.

Let us look at the biblical passages:

1. Matthew 26:26–29

And as they were eating, Jesus took bread, and blessed it, and broke it, and gave it to the disciples and said, "Take, eat; this is my body." Then, taking a cup, he gave thanks, and gave it to them, saying, "Drink of it, all of you; for this is my blood, the blood of the covenant, which is shed for many for the remission of sins. I tell you I shall not drink again of this fruit of the vine until that day when I drink it new with you in my Father's kingdom."

2. Mark 14:22–25

And as they were eating, he took bread, blessed it, broke it, and gave it to them, and said, "Take; this is my body." Then, taking a cup, he gave thanks and gave it to them, and they all drank of it. And he said to them, "This is my blood, the blood of the covenant, which is shed for many. Truly, I say to you, I shall not drink again of the fruit of the vine until that day when I drink it new in the kingdom of God."

The brevity of the two passages may surprise us. Matthew and Mark capture a unique moment and set forth an essential practice in a few phrases. They say almost exactly the same thing; Mark omits the forgiveness of sins, but it is already included in the blood that is shed. They both write with an eloquence that disregards eloquence, repeating the succinct and inexhaustible words of Jesus: "This is my body...This is my blood."

3. Luke 22:19–20

Then, taking bread, he gave thanks, broke it and gave it to them, saying, "This is my body which is given for you. Do this in remembrance of me." And likewise the cup after supper, saying, "This cup is the new covenant in my blood, shed for you."

There are several differences. Luke places Jesus's sentence "For I tell you that from this time on I shall not drink of the fruit of the vine until the kingdom of God comes" (verse 18) later in the evening. He recalls the fact that Jesus had spoken of his body "given" for men (as of his blood shed for them), this gift being already implied in the passages from Matthew and Mark. His formula, "This cup . . . is the new covenant in my blood," seems to use *cup* for *wine* ("this" in Matthew and Mark) metonymically, unless a nuance is escaping me. Above all, he records other words of Jesus, "Do this in remembrance of me," which clearly say that this solemn moment is to be repeated.

We find this repetition, after the death of Jesus, in the Acts of the Apostles, when new disciples are added:

1. Acts 2:42

And they devoted themselves to the apostles' teaching and fellowship, to the breaking of bread and the prayers.

The Lord's supper, at its origin in the paschal meal, is designated by the attractive and familiar expression "the breaking of bread."

2. Acts 2:46

And day by day, with one accord, they attended the temple together and broke bread in their homes, partaking of food with gladness and singleness of heart.

Is it the Lord's supper that is referred to here, or ordinary meals? In the Greek, the verb translated by *broke* has the same root as the substantive translated, in verse 42, by *breaking*.

3. Acts 20:7

On the first day of the week, when we were gathered together to break bread. . . .

The "first day of the week" seems to indicate that it is indeed the Lord's supper; "gathered together to break bread" once again designates this solemn and joyful meal with an everyday expression.

4. Acts 27:35

[Paul] took bread, and giving thanks to God in the presence of all he broke it and began to eat.

After fourteen days without eating, on a drifting boat, Paul convinces the sailors to take some food; he himself eats, and they follow his example. The New Jerusalem Bible's note says that "the terms Luke uses seem to suggest the Eucharist"; indeed, the context speaks of the "saving" of all the sailors by an act of God, an angel having revealed to Paul that no one would perish. The "Eucharist" here resembles to such an extent a simple Jewish meal, in which one gives thanks before breaking the bread, that one hesitates to make the distinction.

Isn't this curious? In examining these passages, think of all that is not found in them. And of all that is.

2.

In reading about the way in which the first Christians lived out the "breaking of bread," we could worry ourselves about a certain gap in relation to most of the celebrations that we have developed since then. In reading the accounts of the Last Supper, we must notice, around the great truths that are revealed to us—especially "This is my body... This is my blood"—a total absence of explanations. Reading Paul vividly illuminates this absence:

1. 1 Corinthians 10:16–17

The cup of blessing which we bless, is it not communion in the blood of Christ? The bread which we break, is it not communion in the body of Christ? Because there is one bread, we who are many are one body, for we all partake of the one bread.

That we commune in the blood and body of Christ is already included in the words of Jesus. Then, through the authority that is given him, Paul draws the already latent lesson from the sharing of the bread that Christians constitute a single body.

2. 1 Corinthians 11:23–26

For I received from the Lord what I also delivered to you, that the Lord Jesus on the night when he was betrayed took bread, and when he had given thanks, he broke it, and said, "This is my body which is [broken] for you. Do this in remembrance of me." In the same way also the cup, after supper, saying, "This cup is the new covenant in my blood. Do this, as often as you drink it, in remembrance of me." For as often as you eat this bread and drink the cup, you proclaim the Lord's death until he comes.

His account of the Last Supper closely resembles that of Luke, which he doubtless influenced. In repeating the words of Jesus, "Do this in memory of me," regarding the blood, he makes manifest what Luke will leave assumed. Even by declaring that the faithful "proclaim" the death of Jesus and by orienting the memorial toward the future ("until he comes"), he makes explicit what the Gospels will only suggest. And here is the essential: he restricts himself to giving the words of Jesus without explaining them. He who, like us, might have been tempted to probe these mysterious sentences, to reason them out, to ask himself, for example, to what extent and by what process the bread and the wine can be the body and blood of Jesus, or if Jesus is found completely in the bread and completely in the wine, and so on—abstains from doing so. He of whom the Holy Spirit could have availed Himself to shed light on these questions and others instead adds nothing. Since even Paul limits himself to transmitting the words that Jesus gave him, so that they shine forth in our hearts and minds, shouldn't we discipline ourselves to listen to them? Let us put ourselves in the place of the twelve, who heard the very words of Jesus and had to be amazed at the gift that he was giving them, without understanding—and perhaps without seeking to understand—how the bread being given to them could be the body of the one who was there among them.

3.

The fact that Paul does not try to elucidate Jesus's words and gestures from the Last Supper doubtless gives us an astonishing and salutary hermeneutical lesson. When he warns the Corinthians not to eat the bread and drink the cup "in an unworthy manner," for they would bring judgment upon themselves by failing to "discern the body [of the Lord]" (1 Corinthians 11:27–29), he focuses attention on the essential, on the necessity of listening to Jesus say to his disciples and to whoever wishes to hear him: "This is my body." He does not explain, he asks to be obeyed.

Not holding to what is written is foolhardy, vain, and potentially dangerous, and the danger is revealed above all when we try to listen to these evangelical and apostolic words regarding the Lord's supper. It is here more than anywhere else that one must become aware of the nature of the books of the Bible, and avoid submitting them to our doubly foreign analyses. It is fitting here to remind ourselves of other words, threatening ones, found at the end of the book of Revelation:

> If any one adds to [the words of the prophecy of this book], God will add to him the plagues described in this book! And if any one takes away from the words of this prophecy, God will take away his share in the tree of life and in the holy city, which are described in this book!
>
> (22:18–19)

Add nothing, and take nothing away: the message recurs often in the Bible, as if in order to warn us of our insatiable will to embellish and to restrict. Here is Moses addressing Israel: "You shall not add to the word which I command you, nor take from it; that you may keep the commandments of the LORD your God which I command you" (Deuteronomy 4:2). Later he says it again: "Everything that I command you you shall be careful to do; you shall not add to it or take from it" (Deuteronomy 13:1). Here is Agur, in Proverbs:

> Every word of God proves true;
> he is a shield to those who take refuge in him.
> Do not add to his words,
> lest he rebuke you,
> and you be found a liar.
>
> (30:5–6)

To add to the Bible is to lie. Moreover, God's words resemble his acts, of which it is said in Ecclesiastes:

> I know that whatever God does, it shall be forever.
> Nothing can be added to it,
> nor anything taken from it;
> and God has made it so, that men should fear before him.
>
> (3:14)

It is just as irreverent, and just as laughable, to modify what he says as to seek to modify what he does. And just as his acts remain, so the Bible, as the word of God, remains unscathed regardless of our alterations and our suppressions. The warning at the end of Revelation is located at the end of the Bible. It forbids, in the first place, the suppression of passages and the insertion of others. But it also teaches us how to approach the biblical writings, by pointing out what I call their "poetic" nature, their resistance to paraphrase.

And yet, all the controversy regarding the subject of the Lord's supper opposes those who add to those who take away. Protestants take away from the strength of the verb in the words "This is my body...This is my blood." Calvin wants to know how the body of Christ can be found at once in both heaven and "under innumerable bits of bread"; the Anglican Church's Book of Common Prayer likewise presumes that the natural body of Christ cannot be "in several places at the same time." The argument would be perfectly reasonable in our world ruled by the (divine) laws of physics, but it is unreasonable to argue in this way about a Being who surpasses us infinitely. The same inappropriate reasoning is used when Calvin draws support from the words of Jesus to his disciples after his resurrection—"See my hands and my feet, that it is I myself; handle me, and see; for a spirit has not flesh and bones as you see that I have" (Luke 24:39)—in order to declare that, according to this definition of what a body is, the body of Jesus cannot be present in the bread because we can neither see it nor handle it. Article 28 of the Anglican Church's Articles of Religion affirms that "the Body of Christ is given, taken, and eaten . . . only after an heavenly and spiritual manner," which amounts to saying that "this is my body," but only in a certain manner. Even Luther insists on reasoning beyond what is disclosed to us. During the Marburg Colloquy, where he debated this question with Zwingli, he wrote on the table HOC EST CORPUS MEUM and refused every effort to translate EST by "represents," "figures," "is the sign of." But he also maintained that the body of Christ is "with, in, and under the bread"—as if we could know that.

4.

The Reformers mistrusted the literal reading of the words "This is my body," considering it to have led the Roman church into error. If we must not remove any of the words of Jesus, Calvin was right to say that we likewise must not, by considering them "rashly, and without choice," deduce from them a whole structure of ideas and practices foreign to those words. Jesus does not restrict the reach of what he gives us by saying, for instance, "This is the figure of my body," but neither does he say, "This becomes my body" or "This is transformed into my body." And nothing in the text authorizes us to think that "This is my body" and "This is my blood" are performatives (like "The meeting is opened"), and that the change is included in the formulas. Adding the notion of bread that *becomes* the body of Christ opens the door to a long series of other additions, which arose so early and are so deeply rooted in custom that they seem natural and obvious to many: the prayer of consecration, for example, during which at a precise moment the bread is "eucharistized"; the necessity that, for the transformation to take place, the words be pronounced by a validly ordained "priest"; the fact of offering the consecrated elements to God, in presuming that "the divine sacrifice ... is celebrated in the Mass," Christ being "offered in an unbloody manner" in a truly "propitiatory sacrifice" (I quote from the Council of Trent as it is reproduced in the Catechism of the Catholic Church).

I call these beliefs to mind not in order to rehash the perfectly well-known arguments that endeavor to show them to be misguided, but simply so that we might stop for a moment in order to see, to begin with, their distance from the Last Supper in the Gospels and the breaking of bread in the Acts of the Apostles and First Corinthians; and second, and above all, in order to recognize our inveterate habit of receiving the Bible not as the word of God that is sufficient unto itself, but as a text to submit to the ingenuity of our reasoning. Jesus said, "Take, eat, this is my body," not, "This is my body, worship." Nor did he say, "This is me." Neither Matthew nor Mark nor Luke shows the disciples adoring the body of Christ in the consecrated bread, before or after eating. The allusions in the Acts of the Apostles to moments in which the first Christians "broke bread" contain nothing that foretells later elaborations, avoiding as they do any opportunity to describe consecration, elevation, adoration, or to point out specifically who was appointed to preside over the rite. Neither does Paul take the opportunity, in reminding the Corinthians of the Last Supper and its continuation in the gathering of Christians, of setting forth the modalities of the rite and of informing his readers that it constitutes a sacrifice.

I hope my Catholic and Protestant friends will understand me. I know the proofs that they would use to refute me, and I am not seeking to win an argument. I ask that all of us who believe that the Bible is the word of God, through a faith that comes not from us but that is a precious gift that we have received from God—that we might read this word without any presuppositions other than this one: that what it says is true. Let's listen to these texts, freeing ourselves from the buzz of all the customary ideas that accompany us in their reading, and which can seem to belong to them. I do not deny the necessity of being vigilant and of examining the way in which it is fitting to understand each word and each series of words. Calvin was not wrong, in principle, to emphasize that one must not take the verb *to be* literally in the formulas of Jesus before reflecting on the question and as if a literal reading were self-evident. When Paul writes, regarding the rock that Moses struck in order to make water flow from it, that "this rock was Christ" (1 Corinthians 10:4), or when Jesus himself says, "I am the gate" (John 10: 7, 9), or "I am the true vine" (John 15:1), we are not required to believe that Jesus is literally a rock, a gate, or a vine. No—but the equivalent of the first example would be, "This bread is me," and of the second and the third examples, "I am this bread." Thinking about the different function of the verb *to be* in these expressions—or better, thinking about the different relation between the person and the object within the verb—warns us rather to avoid lending a meaning to "This is my body" that does not fit. The singular formula encourages us to welcome the depth of the verb *to be* and the fact that the meaning that Jesus gives it is both marvelous and unfathomable. Do we really need to know how the bread "is" the body of the Lord? Here above all, by posing questions that the texts do not answer—Is the substance of the bread annihilated? Do the accidents of the bread and the wine remain? and so on—we play the role of the willing dog faced with Beethoven's quartets. The words of Jesus are clear and secret, clear about the unheard-of gift that is given to us—hear him say to us, "This is my body . . . This is my blood"—and secret because of the transcendence of his divinity. Should we not feel that, through these mysterious expressions, he invites us to open ourselves to the mysteries of being itself, to let ourselves be surpassed by this moment that is at once outside time and at the heart of time? What for us is the past ("Do this in memory of me") and the future ("You proclaim the death of the Lord, until he comes") flows toward the presence of this very special present, where time seems both to accelerate and to be immobilized—or better, where we have the impression of glimpsing, during communion and also when we are transported through the reading of the account to the Last Supper itself, another sort of time, the faint echo (might we say?) of God's "time." Jesus gives us a kind of initiation to being, not in order to satisfy our intellect, but in order to draw us, through faith and love on our side, and, on his, through Love and the power of his word, to him, to his totally other and yet human being. At least that is what I feel. If the words and the gestures of Jesus speak otherwise to the reader, may he deepen them for himself, forgetting what I have written.

5.

I find myself also obliged to respond to another approach to the Lord's supper, because it runs counter to everything I have put forward with regard to the Bible and its reading. It is that of Jean-Luc Marion in *God Without Being*, an impressive book, widely read and commented upon, and justly so. It is less his explanation of communion that troubles me (he offers a very interesting perspective on the Catholic position) than the supposed relation between communion and the texts of the Bible. When he writes, "The Eucharist requires of whoever approaches it a radical conceptual self-critique and charges him with renewing his norms of thought," I can only applaud.[1] But in his reading, essential to his argument, of Jesus's encounter with the "disciples of Emmaus" (Luke 24:13–35), he dangerously diminishes the power of the scriptures by his focus on the Eucharist.

He develops a strong idea there. The two disciples, who have heard about the death of Jesus, cannot understand it. Only Jesus is in a position to explain it, and beginning with Moses he explains to them everything in the scriptures that concerns him. And yet the Gospel does not transcribe this explanation, as Marion writes: "Barely named, it disappears to the benefit of the eucharistic moment."[2] The eucharistic moment "accomplishes . . . the hermeneutic," for it is only when, having arrived at the village, Jesus breaks the bread and gives it to the disciples that their eyes are opened and they recognize him.[3] For Marion, every hermeneutic, which must aim at the Word through the texts, thus finds its site and its end in the "Eucharistic celebration," the only moment in which the Word is really present.

Is this right? Jesus interprets the Old Testament for the two disciples, showing them the passages that announced both his "suffering" and his "glory" (verse 26), but he does the same in the Gospels, where his explanations are given. If he speaks to them of "all the things concerning himself" (*ta peri heautou*, verse 27) in the Hebrew Bible, he had already spoken of these things to the twelve. Soon after the Last Supper, he warned them of his leaving, with these words: "For I tell you that this scripture must be fulfilled in me, 'And he was reckoned with transgressors'; for what is written concerning me [*ta peri emou*] has its fulfillment" (Luke 22:37). He quotes a verse from chapter 53 of Isaiah, which deals precisely with the sufferings and the glory of the "servant" on whom God has laid our faults. Since the Old Testament is veiled to the Jews' sight, it is in part the work of the New Testament to make it legible, and the light does not always come from Jesus. The evangelists constantly affirm that such or such event took place "so that" such and such prophetic announcement "would be fulfilled"; at Pentecost, Peter proclaims the resurrection of Jesus by drawing on two psalms of David (Acts 2:25–28, 34–35); Philip, reading the same passage from Isaiah to the Ethiopian, who is convinced that he could not understand it without guidance, proclaims to him "the good news of Jesus" by "beginning with this scripture" (Acts 8:35). In none of these cases is there any question of the Eucharist.

I mention these well-known verses because Marion seems to place on the same level of incomprehension and explanation the Old Testament and the New. We must transgress the text, he writes, "by the text, as far as to the Word. Otherwise, the text becomes an obstacle to the comprehension of the Word: just as the Old Testament for the disciples, so, for us, the New."[4] It would indeed be good for every Christian teaching constantly to have Christ as its beginning and end. But in the domain that concerns us, the New Testament does not hide, as the Old does, things that await their interpretation, and if Jesus addresses himself to the crowd in parables, he explains them to the disciples. One is led to say that for Marion the text of the New Testament is an obstacle in every case. Jesus as Word, he writes, a Saying, a Said who absolutely transcends human language, because he is "indissolubly speaker, sign, and referent," "is not said in any tongue."[5] In order to say him, our languages would have to speak "as He alone speaks," with authority.[6] Our language is certainly undermined by the consequences of a first linguistic corruption in the mouth of the serpent of Genesis, and of a first disobedience; being human, our language cannot speak with complete adequacy of the Son of God. Our theology, like my resistance to a certain theology, is not based on any authority at all and remains insufficient. But does God not know that better than us? Does not Jesus in his *kenosis* accept saying that he is necessary for our salvation in the only language, poor and mortal, that we have? Above all, didn't the writers of the New Testament write with authority? If Jesus speaks with his own authority (*exousia*, Mark 1:22), Paul declares he has received authority (*exousia*) from this same Lord for the "edification" of the Corinthians through his letters (2 Corinthians 10:8). All scripture, he says in his second letter to Timothy (3:16), is "inspired by God" and *ōphelimos*, profitable.

Concentrating everything on the Eucharist leads Marion to devalue the New Testament, which he claims cannot give access, unlike the Eucharist, to the death and resurrection of Christ. The text of the Gospels, he writes, "does not coincide with the event or permit going back to it, since it results from it.... The text assures us a negative [image] of the event that alone constitutes the original."[7] Easter is a past event, "finite," "foreclosed," of which the text bears only a "trace."[8] "For the disciples [at Emmaus], as for us, it no longer belongs to the present. Once things have happened, there remain only words: for us, there remains the text of the New Testament, just as for the disciples there remained only the rumor, or already the chronicle, of the putting to death."[9] (But it is precisely the New Testament that these disciples did not have. They were "fools" [Luke 24:25] because they did not possess the interpretation of Easter that Jesus hastened to give them, and with which the New Testament provides us.) Because of the gap between text and event, "the text remains so radically non-evential that no salvation can occur in it."[10] Only the Eucharist makes Jesus, dead and resurrected, truly present.

It is true that the New Testament does not actually transport us either to Calvary or to Jesus's appearances after his resurrection, just as the Gospels do not place us, for example, among the crowd listening to the Beatitudes. But we do not need to be present at the events, and no biblical author evokes such an obligation. We know, since Paul affirms it, that faith is reckoned to us as righteousness, just as for Abraham, if we believe "in him that raised from the dead Jesus our Lord, who was put to death for our trespasses and raised for our justification" (Romans 4:24–25). The New Testament, which is not reduced to "words," does not deliver a meaning, does not construct a conceptual system, a structure of thought. Word of God and not human hermeneutical essay, it guides us at every moment to the person of Christ, to the cross and the empty tomb, so that faith may come to us by listening. The reading of the New Testament, like that of the Old Testament, is indeed salutary, as Paul says explicitly to Timothy: the scriptures "are able to instruct you for salvation through faith in Jesus Christ" (2 Timothy 3:15). The letter does not save us, but God speaks to us through his word, and grace can touch us if we read it with a view to understanding it. Reading can itself become an event, above all when Jesus is present and speaks to us. There is no denying the specificity or the unique character of the Lord's supper, but even so Jesus is always present in his infinitude and his love, just as he is in our midst in an objective and particularly sensible way when "two or three" are gathered in his name (Matthew 18:20). His presence is completely real in this gathering and irrefutable, since he speaks the word *eimi*, I am.

6.

I would prefer to celebrate with Jean-Luc Marion all that we have in common instead of writing like this! I am sure that we are in agreement about the fundamental things. Christians in the plethora of contradictory churches adore the same God and have no need of theological formulas in order to live the fraternal communion to which they are called. Arguments will probably not end about the relationship between the Last Supper of Jesus with the twelve and the Jewish Passover meal. But we could perhaps start to see clearly and speak the same language by naming this commemoration the same way the canonical authors do: the Lord's supper, the breaking of bread. The Anglican Church's "Holy Communion" has the merit of attracting attention, by following Paul (1 Corinthians 10:17), to the essential: we commune in the body and blood of Christ, but this *koinōnia* is not strictly speaking the name of the event. Neither is "the Eucharist": the word comes from the Greek verb that is translated as "giving thanks" and testifies to our gratitude, but it emphasizes a single dimension of the act, and it gives it a scholarly halo that corresponds neither to the simplicity of the "supper" nor to the transcendent solemnity of what happens in it. Perhaps I am too fussy; among the other invented words, "host" (victim), which is foreign to the texts, repels and divides.

For so much unites us. Who wrote the following passages?

Christ is the only food of our souls, by which our heavenly Father invites us to him [in the sacrament], that, having eaten our fill of his substance, we may ever and anon gather new vigor until we reach the heavenly immortality.

[Our souls find] their nourishment in Christ. This could not be, did not Christ truly form one with us, and refresh us by the eating of his flesh, and the drinking of his blood.

Let us have this undoubtable confidence, that in taking the sign of the body, we also take the body.

That participation in his flesh and his blood by which Christ transfuses his life into us, just as if he penetrated our bones and marrow, he testifies and seals in the Supper.

Calvin, in the *Institutes* (4.17).[11] This is what he believed, having received it from the Bible, before restricting the scope of this simple belief in order to counter what he considered to be regrettable interpolations. The Anglican Catechism in the Book of Common Prayer likewise affirms that the body and the blood of Christ "are verily and indeed taken and received."

From the other side, read the Jerusalem Bible (my daily reading at the moment) and its notes. A Protestant, an Anglican, finds there everything he believes and nothing that he does not. There is no allusion to the transformation of the elements, to the sacrifice of the Mass, to the priest who offers it, to the adoration of the blessed sacrament. Here is the note on the words "breaking of bread" in Acts 2:42:

In itself the phrase suggests a Jewish meal at which the one who presides pronounces a blessing before dividing the bread. For Christians, however, it implies the eucharistic ceremony.... This, v. 46, was celebrated not in the Temple but in private houses; an ordinary meal would accompany it.

The École biblique de Jérusalem scrupulously translates and faithfully annotates the scriptures, to the point that the arsenal brought to bear by the theologians becomes necessary in order to pass beyond them. If we could settle on reading this version together, there would be no more controversy.

And why do we abstain from repeating Jesus's gestures at the Last Supper? Why not take bread and break it?—as Jesus did according to the accounts of the three synoptic Gospels and according to Paul in 1 Corinthians 11:23–24, and as the first Christians did according to the accounts in Acts and according to Paul, once again, in 1 Corinthians 10:16? If we were breaking and receiving real bread, we would obey Jesus, and we would feel closer to the original event and close to one another. May Catholics and the modern Anglicans who no longer follow the biblical directives of the Book of Common Prayer read these deeply moving and federative texts together. And then would it not also be necessary to drink the wine, because Jesus orders us to do so? "Drink of it, all of you; for this is my blood" (Matthew 26:27–28); "This cup is the new covenant in my blood. Do this, as often as you drink it, in remembrance of me" (1 Corinthians 11:25). The commandment is clear, and sufficient, without any other consideration, for us all to commune in the blood of Christ. Would we not then also have the conviction of rejoining Jesus in this first and eternal meal?

POETRY, DIVINE AND HUMAN

I.

RESPECTING the words of the Bible becomes obligatory once we recognize that the Bible is the word of God. There is no need for us to add our glosses: in remaining faithful to the words, we can endlessly sound their depths.

The Bible invites us to consider the other manifestations of the divine word. Should we not be astonished first of all that God created the heavens and the earth with words: "God said, 'Let there be light,' and there was light" (Genesis 1:3)? He also gave Moses tablets of stone, "written with the finger of God" (Exodus 31:18); and the names of the faithful are "written in the book of life" (Revelation 21:27). Writers, especially playwrights and poets, can rejoice that speech and writing are at work in the creation of the universe and the salvation of humanity—while at the same time accepting that we do not understand the nature of the divine word in Creation any more than we do the relation between the book of life and the books that we compose. Nor do we know by what words God created what we call light, trees, or wild animals, since the author of this passage from Genesis necessarily had recourse to Hebrew, a human language. When God names the light "day," the firmament "heaven," or the mass of water "seas," his language draws close to that of men, yet for all that his names elude us. Placed in the heart of his creation, we are surrounded by his speech and his words, and yet we are not capable of either hearing them or reading them. Here, words and things, a divine language and the presences of a created and named universe, are certainly in perfect harmony, but we do not hear the speech of the universe that responds to the word of God: only through faith do we listen when "the heavens are telling the glory of God," or hear that "day to day pours forth speech,/and night to night declares knowledge" (Psalms 19:1, 2–3).

And what do we hear when we read that Jesus is the Word of God in the Creation, and the Word made flesh in the Incarnation? Our thoughts are probably inept. Nevertheless, would it be admissible to conclude, from the fact that one of the Persons of what we call the Trinity is the Word, that speech, words, language or something that resembles them is found at the heart of divine experience, just as it is in human experience? On the earth the Word spoke continually, according to the Gospels and the beginning of the Acts of the Apostles; he continued to speak from heaven, according to Acts and Revelation; and in these texts he continues to speak to us even now. Like the biblical authors, he employs a human language, which is nevertheless other, and its alterity is clear if we have the grace to hear it. The Word on the cross is surrounded by words at once both human and divine. The evangelists quote the Old Testament: "They divide my garments among them/and for my raiment they cast lots" (Psalms 22:18, Matthew 27:35), "He was numbered with the criminals" (Isaiah 53:12, Mark 15:28), "Not one of them [his bones] is broken" (Psalms 34:20, John 19:36), "They look on him whom they have pierced" (Zechariah 12:10, John 19:37). Jesus reiterates other passages of the psalmists: "I thirst" (John 19:28, Psalm 69:21), "My God, my God, why have you abandoned me?" (Matthew 27:46, Psalms 22:2), "Into your hands I commend my spirit" (Luke 23:46, Psalms 31:6). The experience of Israel and the words of its poets who have transmitted it culminate in the Messiah.

From the Christian point of view, spoken language is found at the same time in the secret of God, infinitely distant from our languages, and at the same time in Hebrew, Greek, French, English, and so on. The Word created the universe, just as the words of the writer make a new and unforeseen world exist. But the relation between the divine word and the human is problematic. God and man have in common the fact that they speak, and speaking perhaps figures among the traits that formed man in the "image" of God: "God *said*: 'Let us make man in our image'" (Genesis 1:26). Language presents itself as a mystery, an invitation to that which transcends it. Even at the purely earthly level, ever since the Fall and specifically after Babel, the capacity of each language, among the thousands that exist, to discover its own world related to all the others but offering a particular perspective, a unique vision of the real, already testifies to the heuristic and creative virtue of language. Whatever the gap between human words and the divine Word, Baudelaire is certainly right to affirm (in his essay on Théophile Gautier) that there is "in the word [*le mot*], in the *word* [*le verbe*] something *sacred* that prevents us from making of it a game of chance."

2.

The poetry of the Bible, coming from God, is thus singular, but before addressing its character, we must reflect anew on the nature of poetry in general, and in the first place on its relation to the Word of God and the Word made flesh. The Word is certainly not made flesh in our poems, and neither are human words. If the life of the poet resonates with the presence of Jesus and the poet succeeds in translating a little of this presence into a poem, perhaps with the conviction that God stimulated and aided him, he nevertheless is not composing a page of scripture. Jesus appears in his text in just as partial a manner as he does in any action motivated by grace and hindered by sin. Human words are already flesh. Their sounds emerge from our mouths and penetrate our ears (even when read in silence), and their rhythms move in our bodies. Thought does not await the poem to become incarnate: it is already incarnated in the person who thinks and in the language of his thought. Rather, what is proper to poetry is the making sensible of the corporal nature of language. Through its concentration and its reluctance to deliver merely a message, a poem invites us into the life of words, directs our attention to the sounds to be heard and the rhythms to be felt. Poetry exists in part in order to reveal the sound and the rhythm of a meaning, the cadence of an emotion, the breath of an idea, the depths of language that relate it to bodies full of mind and to a reality vibrating with logos, with intelligence.

In this perspective, a poem constitutes a very special kind of body. A singular way of speaking, which seems nevertheless to have existed very early in the history of language, it fascinates by its form and the life of its form. In the rigor of its verse, even "free" verse, it seeks to exist as an entity and a unity; it produces its sounds and it breathes like an animal body; and yet its body is not localized, and remains intangible. This body resembles no other body—except that of every work of art. All the arts appear in the form of a strange body. A painting is at the same time *Le Déjeuner sur l'herbe* and a piece of rectangular canvas; a quartet is passion, mathematics, wood, and catgut, unfolding at once here, with the musicians, and nowhere; a dance is human bodies and configurations in space that vanish in the air; even the solidity of an edifice is transposed by the aesthetics of volumes and views. A poem, a body that, like ours, abounds in emotions, thoughts, memories, and words, would be the outline of another sort of body, of what the Bible calls a "glorious body" (Philippians 3:21), or, in the course of an argument at once dense and poetic in the first letter of Saint Paul to the Corinthians, a "spiritual body" (1 Corinthians 15:44). These last words help us understand, through the surprising oxymoron they compose, what I evoked in the first chapter: the Bible does not speak of the mere destruction of the universe, but of the creation at the end of time of "new heavens" and a "new earth" (2 Peter 3:13), and it does not present men as immortal souls that will escape from their bodies in order to be raised into the beyond, but as complex corporal beings who will be transformed and will live, so to speak, here. A poem is absolutely not a spiritual body; it is the glimpse, through its order and its alterity, of this carnal possibility.

One often has the impression while writing or reading a poem of entering an unknown land, and of finding oneself, due to the potentialities of language—above all when it is thus organized, cadenced, *voiced*—at the limits of what one knows and crossing a threshold. Thanks to its unaccustomed body, poetry names the real anew. It continues the task of Adam, consisting in naming the animals, but now in a fallen world, where to rename the real is to re-create it according to the perception that we have of the real, in view of the future or the true re-creation of the world at the end of history. A poem draws the real toward newness and song. A being, an event, an object, approached from another angle and welcomed into the happy play of words, is transformed, and gives onto a world beyond ours. A garden in a village north of London, where we see paths, moss, shadows, and greenery, is transfigured at the moment in which, in the "Ode to a Nightingale," Keats speaks of the light "from heaven . . . with the breezes blown" among "verdurous glooms and winding mossy ways." *Verdurous glooms*, by its strangeness, makes the green shadows more beautiful, renews our perception of the earth, and suggests—merely, and at a great distance—the "new earth." The light of heaven, instead of glowing and fading in the passage of the wind that modifies the reflections in the leaves, moves like the wind, and sketches a real wavering between the palpable and the impalpable, between the sky where the moon reigns and the kingdom of heaven. In our poetry, the real appears otherwise.

The wind shifting the light is an irrational idea, a poetic truth, and an observed fact. While some rashly associate poetry and revelation (God alone can reveal to us what transcends us), the existence of poetry is revelatory. Through its strange body, its modified syntax, its unexpected associations of words, its metaphors and its other creative figures, poetry changes everything it touches; it calls to mind the possibility of a deeper change; it awakens the other within the same. It sees beyond what is offered to the eyes and the intelligence. It does this always, regardless of the convictions, religious or otherwise, of the poet. Just as Jesus, the Word of God, is the royal way by which God enters into his creation and draws near to us, so our poetic word in response translates our fumbling intuition of a different reality. Whence the old tradition that poetry in its very nature is inspired, and the poet enjoys a privileged access to the realm of the gods or of God by virtue of his condition as *vates*, a prophet born with special intuitions. Poetry has always seemed mysterious (except when it is reduced to a technique that obeys certain rules, or to an involuntary expression of economic, social, or cultural forces), and the poet certainly may believe him or herself "inspired" in the sense that he or she does not entirely master the act of writing. The poet understands that the things he feels and the words he employs come in part from elsewhere. The poet, when he is working well, is at the same time blind and clairvoyant. One learns, in writing and in reading poetry, the complexity of self-knowledge, and one sees that the *I* escapes us. Poetry is revelation only to the extent that the poet reveals something through where he has been, what he has seen, and the strangeness of what has been given to him to discover. If our body changes for the better in the breathing and the perfect movement of the poem, our emotions, our perceptions, our ideas, our entire inner life, inseparable from our outer life, are transformed in the elsewhere of the poem.

3.

Language seems to translate the feeling that there is an intimate link between our body and everything that constitutes us. In Hebrew, the *hand* indicates power, the *face*, presence; in Greek, the *bowels* are the seat of the affections; in English and in many other languages, the affections are born in the *heart*. Naturally incarnate, we are less a soul in a body (often considered a prison) than a body in a soul. We hope for the resurrection of the body (and not for a liberation from our body), and meanwhile, and apparently forever, Jesus is incarnated in us, all Christians being members of the body of Christ (Ephesians 5:30). A poem offers under a different viewpoint our body and all that which contains it: the mind of the poem is not exactly that of the poet, since he writes in part something other than what he was planning, and the body of the poem is of a different nature than his own. In the unusualness of what is said and the way of saying it, our mind and our body change perceptibly.

Which seems to signify that poetry is not essentially a *poiēsis*, the fabrication of an object. Of course, the poet does indeed produce a work, for in writing and revising he seeks the completeness, the precision, and the finish without which the emotions and ideas of the poem, being out of focus, would not have been discovered and would not be fully present, just as the body of the poem would be flabby and clumsy. And yet, the fundamental act of the poet and the fundamental *work* of the poem happen at another level. This does not require us to disdain, like Valéry, the finished poem and instead favor the study of its genesis, for the reason that the poem teaches us much less about the functioning of the human mind than do the seductive complications in the way in which it came to exist. No; the poem introduces not so much a new work as a new experience. If while writing, the poet finds another within himself and something other within the real, as the poem attains its proper form, the right language, and the cadences and sounds that belong to it, then the reader of the finished poem finds in himself an unexpected capacity, and in the real an unforeseen possibility. In the case of Christian poetry, the reading of the poem can constitute a spiritual experience, not because the poet was truly inspired as scripture is, but because the making of a poem resembles every action of a Christian and has perhaps benefited from the same grace. One draws profit from a Christian poem just as from any act of charity, of humility, or of forgiveness.

The singular body of the poem, while acting in time, draws us equally toward the timeless. I see nothing to add here to what T. S. Eliot says in the third of his *Four Quartets*, "The Dry Salvages," except that we must read attentively what he has to say about the Incarnation. Our curiosity, he writes, searches the past and the future, but it is in the present, lived fully and well, that our salvation takes place. He writes that to apprehend "the point of intersection of the timeless / With time" would be "an occupation for the saint," who knows that a different world beats within this one—that each instant is open to the eternal, each place to the infinite—and who must live the presence of God here and now, "in a lifetime's death in love." Most of us only feel "the impossible union / Of spheres of existence" in certain moments "in and out of time":

> The distraction fit, lost in a shaft of sunlight,
> The wild thyme unseen, or the winter lightning
> Or the waterfall, or music heard so deeply
> That it is not heard at all, but you are the music
> While the music lasts.

The signs of a transcendent order arise in the natural world, but also in art: if God lavishes them on creation, he also invites us to discern them in the different forms of art that we have been led to conceive. By finishing his thought with, "The hint half guessed, the gift half understood, is Incarnation," Eliot does not assume that music, or any other form of art, achieves the Incarnation. He simply suggests, but with great audacity, that all moments of vision, whether we are listening to a quartet or a waterfall, allow for the apprehension, far off, of "the impossible union" of God and man in Jesus, the inter-section of the divine and human spheres of existence in a Galilean God. The poem (to come back to language) would be at once both plunged in time and open to the timeless, like Jesus—but this "like" is so inadequate! The disturbing strangeness of the poem's body, so different from our own and yet, just like ours, filled with words, knows how to translate the salutary allusion to the Incarnation with a special strength.

4.

What then of biblical poetry, and of its relation to our poetry? If our human words are mysteriously tied to Jesus, the divine Word, we must assume a much more intimate relationship between Jesus as Word of God and the Bible, also the word of God. It is fitting to recognize, from the beginning, that here we are advancing across a terrain full of hazards. Nevertheless it seems legitimate to think that, just as Jesus is at once both perfectly divine and perfectly human, so biblical poetry and prose are at the same time human and divine. In works written in Hebrew, Aramaic, and Greek, our words and the words that come from God touch and mingle. In holding with Paul that "all scripture is inspired by God" (is "God-breathed," 2 Timothy 3:16), it is likewise possible to believe that in each biblical writing the words were chosen by the author. That the words come from God implies, as I wrote, that it is the very words that count, and that every paraphrase leads us away from them. The words of God were made flesh, by taking residence in the sounds, rhythms, and the appearance of human words. A biblical poem presents itself as a truly spiritual body, a glimpse, infinitely closer than that of a purely human poem, of the spiritual body into which, at the end of time, the bodies of men, and perhaps the earth itself, will be transformed.

That the words come just as much from human beings invites us to reflect seriously on each writer's act of writing, on his manner of being and his relationship to language; and to study the biblical writings—without in any way renouncing our faithfulness to the scriptures—with all the customary rigor of literary study. Poets often have the impression of not being alone in the act of writing, as if sometimes an other, or an unknown region of the self, stepped in to give them the essential emotions, ideas, and words. It is likely that, for the biblical authors, this impression was even stronger, that everything they drew from their own experience was nevertheless given to them, and that their words, chosen with precision, their carefully formed phrases, at the same time came to them from elsewhere. Should we imagine a psalmist, or the author of the book of Job, or of the Song of Songs, hesitating, going back over a certain image or a certain adjective, crossing out badly done passages, worrying when the verses won't come, and ultimately rejoicing at what he wrote? I think so: his natural doubts and pleasure render the human dimension of divine words completely real.

But we should never confuse biblical poetry with that composed outside the Bible, by Christians whose holiness astounds us. The beauty of biblical poetry derives from our drawing near to God and God's drawing near to us in those miraculous words. Divine words and human words are reconciled, and a passage opens between God and us, between us and God. Here there is truly a "point of intersection of the timeless / With time"; "the impossible union / Of spheres of existence" is realized.

5.

The poem, as a body of a special sort, represents the rough sketch of another body, the sign of the transformed body. And if the body of the poem is mysterious, it suggests that the body of the world, the effect of the word of God, is likewise so, and that it too opens to that which transcends it. The strange body of the poem corresponds to the strange body of the material, and more than material, world. In this perspective, all poetry is metaphysical, the whole universe is metaphysical, and appears as a created and living presence, overflowing with words of God, endlessly testifying to the present absence of God the Creator and to its own future condition.

This testimony is poetic, as are these allusions that attend us everywhere, and this is probably because God is the greatest of poets, being at the origin of poetry, and of all forms of art. The light, which allows us to see, remains almost always invisible. The first of God's creatures, the light is clearly both real and other. Two biblical passages, themselves filled with poetry, underscore its singular nature. The Gospel of John, having presented Jesus as the Word through whom everything was created, affirms that the life in him was the light, and that this light shines in the darkness (John 1:3–5). The words resonate with many meanings, and with the back and forth among them. They evoke Jesus, the spiritual light that shines in the darkness of the human condition; the light of the beginning shining in the original darkness; and our own days, which, occurring amid the succession of nights, speak both of Genesis and of Jesus. After the Flood, God made a covenant with all living creatures and chose the sign of the rainbow (Genesis 9:12–17). A perfectly natural phenomenon, the rainbow also has the numinous ability to reveal the light, to render it, in the fitting form of a fragile curve of almost magical colors, suddenly visible.

Or think of the wind, equally invisible, revealed only by its passage through the leaves or on the water's surface, and sharing the same name in Hebrew and in Greek with breath and spirit, which are indispensable to our physical and religious life. Think also of fire, which seems to lead its own life, material and immaterial, and which the biblical authors associate with God. In the book of Deuteronomy, God comes as a "devouring fire" (Deuteronomy 4:24); John the Baptist warns his listeners that Jesus will baptize them "with the Holy Spirit and with fire" (Matthew 3:11); for Paul, Jesus when he returns will inflict vengeance on his enemies in the midst of a "flaming fire" (2 Thessalonians 1:8).

We shouldn't see mere metaphors here, useful means for expressing and making memorable things difficult to grasp: calling Jesus "light" because he illuminates our path, or describing the irruption of the Holy Spirit or the punishment inflicted by God as "fire" because of the suddenness or the violence of such events. Rather, we are in the presence of the poetry of the real. Light, wind, fire, all natural phenomena, brush against the invisible and open this world to another that, always present, suffuses it, but to which we are insensible most of the time. We move among the figures of another reality. These phenomena make us feel that all that is material gives onto the immaterial; our words, through their relation to the Word of God and to God's words, lead us there.

Moses's encounter with God in the burning bush provides an example. This unique bush burns without ever being consumed as the sign of the presence of a different world within the familiar world. But each and every bush invites us, like Moses, to "turn aside" (Exodus 3:3), having been created and, like all of creation, burning with the imprint of God. Every bush comes from the Word of God; a poem taking a bush as its subject can represent our response—that of a fallen Adam—in human words to this divine word, and our effort to rename the bush, to re-create it in the particular life of the poem, to open it, feeble though we are, to its future.

In each synoptic Gospel there exists a passage in which a more-than-corporal body appears, and where the author dips into the resources of poetry in order to describe it. The Transfiguration reveals to three privileged persons a spiritual and glorious body. Luke states that Jesus's face became "other" (*heteron*) and his clothing "dazzling white" (Luke 9:29), Matthew that his face "shone like the sun" and his clothes appeared "white as light" (Matthew 17:2), and Mark that his clothes were "glistening, intensely white, as no fuller on earth could bleach them" (Mark 9:3). The evangelists make recourse to comparisons in order to seize and transmit the unprecedented nature of the alterity become visible. By concentrating on whiteness, the union of all the colors in a world that overflows with them, they seem to suggest that a glorious body possesses, with its transcendence, all the qualities of the body of the world. Mark's declaration, which states that such a whiteness is beyond the reach of human effort, lets us reflect that ordinary whiteness, already the immaculate fullness of absent color, offers on the earth a discrete glimpse of what will be.

The intuition of another world discernable in this one can of course arise outside poetry. It surprises all those who, so to speak, live poetically, ceaselessly conscious of a different presence, within themselves, around them, and in others. Certainly for many this presence does not indicate God but "the transcendent," "the sacred," "the numinous," "the divine," or any attractive abstraction that does not require supposing the existence of a personal God, with a will different from ours. Only grace is able to transform the vision of a different reality into the feeling of the presence of God. This should remind us that the most ardently Christian poetry often produces the same stimulating but incomplete effect. The reader *may* feel, when listening to Péguy, or Agrippa d'Aubigny, that their words brush against the Word and that God draws near; but what the reader experiences can also turn out to be worldly, aesthetic, emotive, or moral.

Which brings me back to the Incarnation, the locus of every reflection on the permeability of our world, fallen though it is, to the presence of another. If the Incarnation must not encourage us to think that our poems constitute, by analogy or in some other way, the Word made flesh, it certainly encourages the writing of poetry. So does the creation: it invites us to respond with new words to the words of God that we "hear" in the real. The Old Testament already contains, in Isaiah's prophecy (Isaiah 65:17), this promise of "new heavens" and a "new earth" upon which the vocation of poetry can be based: seeking beyond the known and at the same time unceasingly exploring the inexhaustible profusion of the known, of given reality. And yet the Incarnation is the true beginning of this newness. At the first Creation, "darkness was covering the deep and the Spirit of God was moving over the waters" (Genesis 1:2). With the Incarnation in sight, the angel says to Mary, "The Holy Spirit will come upon you, and the power of the Most High will overshadow you" (Luke 1:35). The Word taking flesh, the most wondrous sign of the fact that God is with us, immanent as well as transcendent, inaugurates the new Creation at the moment when the Word begins to speak in a new way. If we are astounded that God created the world by saying it, we could also surprise ourselves that the "Word" of God, rather than, for example, the "Son of God," was made flesh, before realizing the pertinence of this new Word. The singular Event prompts poets in particular, and doubtless all workers of the word, to praise and to re-create the world as best they can, with the means available, in anticipation of the infinitely more glorious Re-creation to come.

THE PSALMS, POETRY OF FAITH

I.

MOST READERS know the Psalms only in translation. We do not come into contact with these poems as they were written, we do not read the word made flesh in the body of Hebrew. At best, we follow the development of the sentences in a word-for-word translation, and we seek out the shades of meaning for each term in a dictionary. This is not how we read Keats, or Donne, and this exclusion could sadden us. How can we hear the sounds that respond and contrast? How can we feel the rhythm that bears and creates emotion? How can we hear the memory of the words within the history of the language?

If we think that the Psalms are poems like any other, and as irremediably foreign (unless we immerse ourselves for years in the study of Hebrew) as Chinese, Persian, or Finnish poems, there is nothing to add. However, if we believe that they convey, in one way or another, the word of God, concentrating human and transhuman experience in order to contribute to our well-being, it must be supposed that their translation is not a mere expedient, a necessary albeit regrettable remedy. As with the whole of the Bible, the translation of the Psalms was foreseen; it was in some way part of the program.

This does not mean that the task of the translator is limited to extracting a "message" from the mass of the Hebrew, a meaning expressible in prose, under the pretext that poetry has no relation to salvation, and that all poetry is merely a pleasing means to render a teaching acceptable. But *why* does the "message" appear in a poem? The question remains pertinent: If one wants to express and deepen one's faith, why write a poem, with all the apparently superfluous strictures that it implies (but also with the additional possibilities that this innovative production of language offers)? And why does the author of Psalm 33 exhort the faithful not only to praise God with stringed instruments, but to play "skillfully" and "with loud shouts" (verse 3)? In Psalm 92, the psalmist seems even to reflect on the art that it is fitting for him to bring to bear as poet and perhaps also as musician: "It is good ... to sing praises ... upon an instrument of ten strings and upon the harp" (verses 2–4). He understands that the poetry that he is ready to write and the music that will complete it arise from what is "good," this *tov* that, according to Genesis, was the essential property of light, of the earth, of the sea, and of all of what God's art created. He understands that the poetic act brings him close to this first world, lost but still visible, the whole of which was "very good." Writing a psalm is not about finding the most agreeable way of articulating certain emotions and thoughts. To read or sing a psalm is to be impregnated, even unconsciously, with the presence of art and its capacity to form and to perfect what one feels. What is it that touches us in the Psalms, even in translation, to the point of moving all of our being, if not certain mysterious images, certain rhythms that lift us up? "The heavens declare the glory of God; and the firmament sheweth his handiwork" (Psalm 19:1); "Deep calleth unto deep at the noise of thy waterspouts" (Psalm 42:7); "Out of the depths have I cried unto thee" (Psalm 130:1) ... The task of the translator remains that of every translator of poetry: to dive into the language of each poem, "to listen," as Henri Meschonnic writes in *Gloires*, "to what this language does, and how," and to find in his own language resources of rhythm and sound capable of animating what would be, without them, a mass of words, where the voice that speaks labors to make itself heard.

2.

The poetry of the Psalms is not mere clothing, and their beauty is not simply an ornament. If one accepts the universe as a divine creation, its beauty is essential, inseparable from its being. If Zion, according to Psalm 50, manifests the "perfection of beauty" (verse 2), we understand that beauty does not concern aesthetics alone, but belongs to Zion. Because I don't read Hebrew, I can speak of the beauty of the Psalms only in terms of elements that at first sight are the least attractive and the most difficult to interpret. Take, for example, the seven occurrences of the expression "the voice of the LORD" in Psalm 29. We hear, as it were, the repeated crashing of thunder, which sounds "over the waters," "breaks the cedars," "shakes the deserts," and we feel, through this accumulation, through these varied repetitions, the superhuman force of these natural events and of the God who rules them. The seven returns of the same contribute as well to the structure of the poem, so that its forward movement is accommodated in a form that holds together, and these repetitions suggest, through the resonances of the number seven, perfection and plenitude. The Lord's Prayer also contains seven repetitions, three concerning God and four concerning men: the most elevated prayer has a satisfying and meaningful form. God's intervention in the world reveals an order that transcends us.

The *alphabetical* poems seem to disrupt poetry through an apparently gratuitous artifice consisting of beginning each verse with the twenty-two successive letters of the Hebrew alphabet. We are tempted to mutter, "Why bother?"; above all with regard to Psalm 119, where the eight verses of each of the twenty-two stanzas begin with the same repeated letter. But this psalm praises divine Law, an object of wonder for the poet, to be endlessly pondered and to be tasted like honey (verse 103), and a perfect order to which our disorderly life must aspire. Our life will not attain that order, but the poem that speaks of it, by seeking to make itself worthy of the Law through its own equally severe and deeply joyful order, offers a small glimpse of this harmonious moral and spiritual beauty. The seriousness of the poet is also revealed in the fact that he understands that even the craftsmanship of his poem, at first glance flawless and complete, remains inadequate: "I have seen the limits of all perfection, / but your commandment is without bounds" (verse 96).

The poem's strength passes through its form; the form and the poem are one, like the mountain and its beauty. And the form did not appear to the psalmists as merely a question of technique. They could express their faith in prose; but through poetry they sound its depths, they uncover what it consists of in the very act of writing. For the reader, too, each psalm's form reveals faith, thanks to the emotions and the realizations of the real that take shape, and the astonishing images, metaphors, and comparisons that re-create the world before the eyes of the imagination. (I shall return to this.) And poetry, without being superior to prose, immediately presents itself as a version of language that is more finely wrought and more self-conscious, just as song—the psalter implies it everywhere—without being superior to poetry, fulfills speech. In permeating ourselves with poetry, in penetrating its domain by leaving behind us the prose of our daily life, we cross a threshold, we find ourselves amid the strange. Every poem makes us slip into the extraordinary, but the Psalms, like all biblical poetry, show us, if we share the faith that undergirds them, the exact reason for this feeling of unfamiliarity. By listening to their speech, their renewed language that renews the world, we understand, at a distance, the word by which God created the heavens and the earth, not like a sculptor who fashions, but like a poet who speaks, who *says* "Let there be light."

The supposed redundancy of poetry, its apparent triviality in rela-tion to faith, grace, and love, disappears as soon as one evokes speech. If Baudelaire reminds us that there is, in the word, something "sacred," the Psalms remind us of it from within a culture that gave us that startling image of a creator God whose speech is revealed as performa-tive, in the most absolute sense of the word. The image is not exclusive: Psalm 8 considers the heavens as the work of his "fingers" (verse 4). But this is a figure (we assume) for conceiving of the creative action of God, while the vision of a God who created an entire universe by speaking corresponds, for those who believe in it, to the simple truth, sanctioned in the New Testament by the revelation of the God-Word.

Hence the orality of the Psalms, which are offered to readers to be sung. The author of Psalm 33 exhorts the faithful to sing to God "a new song" (verse 3); the expression, which often recurs in the psalter, shows that the psalmists recognize a singular responsibility: that of composing poems apt to enrich praise and to invent original ways of understanding and expressing faith. Next, he evokes the heavens created by the "word" of God and the host of stars by "the breath of his mouth" (verse 6), thinking most likely of both the resemblance and the infinite difference between the act of God and his own, and agreeing that poetry comes forth from the lungs and the mouth of the poet and is addressed to the ear and to the entire body of the reader or listener. This is the moment to recall that the ancient Hebrews (like other peoples?) read, as far as we know, aloud, and thus *heard* writing, and did not engage it only with their eyes. We are situated at the end of a likely evolution that, beginning with reading aloud, has passed through silent reading accompanied by a movement of the lips, to end up in a mental reading, where the body, most often slumped in a chair, is almost absent.

Hence also the insistence with which the psalmists return to evil speech, to speaking as the source of evil: the mouth of the wicked man "is filled with cursing and deceit and violence; / under his tongue are mischief and iniquity" (Psalm 10:7). If God is the Word, speech touches our being, for good or ill, and the poets of the psalter, if they know the book of Genesis, must reflect on it when writing their own words. Which above all leads, it seems to me, to their way of evoking death. They conceive of the sojourn of the dead as a terrible silence, where the wicked cannot speak (31:18), and where no one can "praise the LORD" (115:17). Death is privation of the God who speaks, descent into a complete silence where one can neither speak to nor hear him. The idea disturbs them, and affects them as poets. In death, they think, speech will be refused them, while in life on earth they know they are in contact with the mystery of language.

3.

Just as we all are. The poets of the Psalms feel in a reflective way what others feel without necesssarily thinking about it. So it is interesting to study how they live their vocation and learn to know themselves better, and above all to know better the God in whose service they write, but also the world that they are constantly exploring. On the one hand, they are quite conscious of being poets: they feel the joy and the responsibility of the gift that inhabits them. "My mouth is filled with thy praise," affirms the author of Psalm 71 (verse 8), happy to discover in himself a profusion of resources for praising God, and doubtless happy to know that his faith is overflowing with wonder. If I forget Jerusalem, declares the author of Psalm 137, "may my right hand forget!" (verse 5)—may it forget its ability, may the author no longer be able to write poems if he neglect the essential. We are moved when encountering such vocation-worthy engagement at the core of one of the most beautiful psalms, in which the poet weeps with the other captives "by the waters of Babylon" (verse 1), and where his genius shows itself in this hand that might forget in order to punish the mind that forgets, and in another image, particularly terrible to a poet who sings: "Let my tongue cleave to the roof of my mouth" (verse 6). And notice how the poet of Psalm 57 understands his poetic act: "Awake, my soul!/Awake, O harp and lyre!/I will awake the dawn!" (verse 8). He describes better than anyone the moment in which one is seized by the need to praise and to write or to make music, in which one feels all one's being ready to awaken, and language or musical notes ready to be put to work, and in which one desires, through the rightness, the truth, and the newness of what one is creating, to awaken the real, to watch it move in a new way and advance toward its future. In every successful poem, the I and the world awaken, but David arrives at this creative joy after a long descent into anguish (he is assailed by enemies); he evokes a triple awakening that encompasses the poet, his instrument, and the effect of his work on the world, and he arrives at this complete poetics through the irresistible desire to praise.

On the other hand, the act of writing brings the psalmists out of their personal preoccupations, the little circle of the self. Psalm 18, also attributed to David, is filled from one end to the other with affairs of the king, but David not only tells of all that has happened to him during his victorious struggle against his enemies from the perspective of God's saving acts, but he contemplates in memory and with the help of a clairvoyant imagination—about which I shall speak later—God's sublime presence in the presences of nature, and he frequently interrupts himself in order to speak directly to God. His tale of adventure is thus transformed, from the beginning, into an impersonal, or better, a transpersonal work, as it is offered to the choirmaster and destined to become, in the singing of the faithful, the community's poem in music.

The praise that inflames the psalmists leads them toward God and at the same time toward his creation, toward an immense alterity transcending them. Their self is transfigured thanks to the wonder that seizes them before the Creator and before all that he continues to create and to sustain. They give themselves to the world. There is the example, so extraordinary, of Psalm 104:

> The trees of the LORD are watered abundantly,
> the cedars of Lebanon which he planted.
> In them the birds build their nests;
> the stork has her home in the fir trees.
> The high mountains are for the wild goats;
> the rocks are a refuge for the badgers.
>> (Psalm 104:16–18)

Or farther on:

> Yonder is the sea, great and wide,
> teeming with creatures innumerable,
> living things both small and great.
> There go the ships,
> and Leviathan which you did make to play therein.
>> (Psalm 104:25–26)

In the precision of the gaze—the stork in the fir trees, the wild goats (or ibex) on the steep slopes, and in the immense image-filled vision of the earth that God has "covered with the deep as with a garment" (Psalm 104:6)—one feels that the poet's joy before the created world enters into his praise for the Creator, and enriches his love. The idea that God placed the sea monster in the sea "to play therein"—or perhaps "to play with it"—allows us to see the poet's robust tenderness toward the playful pleasure of the whales and other creatures, and his conviction that God also takes pleasure in his creation, not from afar but close up, and at every instant. And so by rejoicing in creation, he imitates God, as verse 31 proclaims: "May the Lord rejoice in his works!" From the point of view of a religious poet, the world that he lives in is not some sort of transparent pane allowing his faith to glimpse divine sovereignty; the world is the dwelling place of his faith, and, in a manner that eludes all of our analyses, the dwelling place of God.

Furthermore, the poet leaves behind his self—or he can do so, and the psalmists certainly do—through the simple act of writing. Why *write* a supplication, for example, as in the many psalms in which the author asks God to come to his aid, to forgive him, or not to forget him? What is the difference between crying out, because the words have been torn from you, "My God, my God, why have you abandoned me?" and composing a poem (Psalm 22) to say it? In the first case, one reacts from inside the emotion, even if one's attention is fixed on the other; in the second, one separates oneself to some degree, however slight, from one's emotion, or better: one brings into play another part of consciousness, which considers the emotion so as to transform it in view of a poem. Once the poem is finished, with the true words, sounds, and rhythms that have progressively imposed themselves, one discovers, with more exactitude than at the beginning, what one is feeling, and in what context the emotion takes its place. The reader receives a certain emotion—that of the poem rather than that of the poet, which remains conjectural—with the depths that the poem confers upon it and with the ramifications that the act of composition has imagined and found.

He thus learns to know himself better. Who speaks in the Psalms? We think, idly, of David, or Asaph, or of an anonymous poet, but the psalmists efface themselves in order to write for the voice of others. Who says, or sings, "Against you, you only, have I sinned" (Psalm 51:6)? Neither David, nor I, nor you; all of us at once. (In the same way, who speaks in the "Ballade des pendus" by François Villon? Who says, "Human brothers who after us live on"?) Another voice often makes itself heard in the course of the poem; every poet can feel that a voice different from his own enters, from time to time or always. The author of Psalm 81 seems to describe quite plainly this curious phenomenon. He begins by encouraging Israel to shout for joy, to sound various instruments to celebrate the feast day; then, after having evoked Joseph and Egypt, he writes: "I hear a tongue I had not known" (verse 6). Indeed, the voice of God suddenly breaks forth, not in response to the poet's enthusiasm, but, by recalling the Exodus, to condemn the waywardness of his people and to declare the happiness that Israel could know if only it obeyed him. The poet disappears, having yielded to this other unexpected voice, which poses rigorous conditions on the outburst of joy that he felt inside of him.

The person at the origin of a psalm becomes other in the act of writing, thus allowing a voice so profound to come through that one perceives it as the voice of man, and sometimes even as the voice of God. From the religious point of view, the poets of the Psalms know in a strong and concentrated way the loss and the re-creation of the self that constitute, ideally, the daily experience of the Christian. From the point of view of poetics and of poetry in general, they clarify and deepen the adventure of every poet: that of not knowing where the words come from, of feeling that another self intercedes. They discover that their poetic act allows, as it were, God to speak. And if they are absent from their poems so as to make a voice heard that is not simply theirs, they nevertheless remain present as guilty and weak people. Psalm 19 is known for the brilliance of its opening: "The heavens are telling the glory of God; / and the firmament proclaims his handiwork"; for its unforgettably evocative images of the created world; and for its celebration of the divine law. And yet the poet, after contemplating things that are far more important than his person, then recalls his fallen condition and the troubling fact that he cannot know all his faults. He asks forgiveness for his hidden faults (Psalm 19:12). He does not write seeking to escape from the labyrinth of the self by assuming an objective stance, and so avoid a reckoning with who one is. Objectivity, like enthusiastic praise, can mask the problem of the self. He expresses himself at once as believer and as poet in the famous prayer that concludes the psalm: "Let the words of my mouth and the meditation of my heart / be acceptable in your sight, / O LORD, my rock and my redeemer" (Psalm 19:14).

4.

Praise is nevertheless central in the psalter. Studying it helps us to position ourselves better in relation to the whole of reality, and to gain a better understanding of poetry. Praise is not the only concern of the Psalms, whose authors are well aware that they inhabit a fallen world where God is equally present and absent, where he "hides" himself (Psalm 10:1, Psalm 13:1) and continually demands that we seek him, but where he also "visits" man (Psalm 8:5) and does not forget him. The Psalms often constitute a cry directed to a God of anger and of mercy. And yet, so often they burst into praise, even after delivering themselves of painful feelings of guilt or abandonment. But once again, why praise God in *poems*? The answer comes through reading and listening to what is said as the poet must be listening to it, without introducing the notion of any sort of "artistic license." Contemplating the heavens that "proclaim the glory of God," the author of Psalm 19 looks with the eyes of faith as well as imagination; he *sees* that God has "set a tent" for the sun (verse 5), that the sun "delights like a bridegroom coming forth from his room," rejoicing like a "hero" to "run its course" (verse 6). Such images convey the wonder that he feels before the sun and its splendor, the youthful vigor of its apparent movement through the skies, as well as his wonder at a God capable of creating it. The poetry participates in the worship and fulfills it. The psalmists do not simply endeavor to praise the best they can but as perfectly as possible, so that the joy that they feel is fully expressed and exists fully, and so that creation too is fully appreciated.

Most remarkably of all, the psalmists exhort all men and women and all creation to praise God. Men and women, sure—but creation? At the end of Psalm 96, which exhorts all the peoples to sing a new song in God's honor, the poet turns to the universe, and summons the "heavens" and "the earth" to rejoice, "the sea and all that fills it" to roar (verse 11), "the field and everything in it" to be exultant, and "all the trees of the wood" to be joyful (verse 12). At the end of Psalm 98, the rivers are invited to "clap their hands" and the mountains to "sing for joy" (verse 8). In Psalm 148, especially, the poet desires to hear the hymn of the entire universe. He calls on the angels and the heavenly multitude to praise God, along with the sun, the moon, and the luminous stars, and he continues,

> Praise the Lord from the earth
> you sea monsters and all deeps,
> fire and hail, snow and frost,
> stormy wind fulfilling his command,
> mountains and all hills,
> fruit trees and all cedars,
> beasts and all cattle,
> creeping things and flying birds
> ....
> Praise the name of the LORD.
>
> (Psalm 148:7–13)

One must read the whole poem to feel the poet's momentum, the ardor with which he addresses in turn all the elements of creation, from the angels to the snow. He seizes the immense multiplicity of beings and things, discerning the whole in which they blend together perfectly in praise.

According to other Psalms, the natural presences are already singing. At the end of Psalm 65, for example,

The pastures of the wilderness drip,
and the hills gird themselves with joy.
The meadows are clothed with flocks,
and the valleys decked with grain,
they shout their joy and they sing.

(Psalm 65:13–14)

This is not a reverdi, as in European medieval poetry, where the
poet's joy projects itself into nature, and where the song of the spring
is that of the birds. For Psalm 19, also attributed to David, begins in
this way:

The heavens are telling the glory of God,
and the firmament proclaims his handiwork.
Day to day pours forth speech,
and night to night declares knowledge.

(Psalm 19:1–2)

Day and night, created by the word of God, speak in their way,
without words, and speak to each other of the glory of the Creator.
Is this a "poetic" way of writing, an agreeable fiction, an anthropo-
morphism that it would be fitting to translate into more prosaic and
rational terms? In the story of the Exodus in Psalm 114, how should
we understand the evocation of the sea that looks and flees, the Jordan
that turns back, mountains that skip like rams and hills like lambs
(verses 3–4)? I would like to think, quite simply, that the psalmists
have reason to write in this way because they *see* better than us the
life that animates all things, they *hear* the joy of creation, they feel
that even the world that we call material has its own manner of being,
its own way of reacting to the presence of God. To address oneself,
as in Psalm 148, to the hail, the winds, and the mountains is to enter
also into a transitive relationship with all that surrounds us, by meta-
morphosing one's self-consciousness through an incessant conscious-
ness of the real and, according to the specificity of the Psalms, of God.

Paul heard the whole of creation "groaning," like a woman in labor (Romans 8:22). David heard the heavens "telling" the glory of God. David is conscious of all that remains of the world of origin despite the Fall; Paul, of the distress that has spread through the whole world ever since. Nevertheless, Paul's image remains the more joyful, because it assumes a world to come, that will fulfill the ternary dynamic of history: from the Creation to the Fall and then to the new Creation, from happiness to misery and then to joy, from life to death and then to resurrection.

5.

The psalmists' poetry is not separate from their faith, and their faith is enriched by their poetic vision of themselves, of the world, and of God. It is in part their imagination that discerns the presence of God in visible reality. In Psalm 29, the voice of God makes itself heard in the storm, it rules over the sea, strikes the trees, divides the flames of fire, makes the desert shake. The Hebrews are clearly not exercising that kind of religious sensibility that considers each natural phenomenon as the sign or even the dwelling of one of the gods. However, would it be sufficient, in order to avoid superstition, to think that for the psalmist thunder is the voice of God only by metaphor—that he gives us merely a small sample of God's power? No, for the poet who *imagines* in this way has perhaps grasped that the omnipresent God who watches over the smallest events of our daily life (Jesus will speak later, in the same tradition, of the death of a sparrow, Matthew 10:29) shows himself in a perceptible manner in thunder, that his terrible voice demands, as the psalmist says, that we prostrate ourselves. (The lightning that, at night, illuminates the whole countryside can produce a similar effect, with that momentary and almost supernatural light, that unusual way of seeing that it creates.) Moreover, in Psalm 18 we pass from a clearly metaphorical poetry to a visionary one. At the beginning, the poet affirms that God is his "rock," his "fortress," his "shield" (verse 3), while death entangles him with its "cords" and sets

a "snare" for him (verse 6). We understand right away that he is work-
ing in a figurative, not literal, vein—although for an ancient Hebrew
such a distinction was perhaps not so clear cut. But everything changes
when he evokes God's intervention:

> He bowed the heavens and came down,
> thick darkness was under his feet;
> he rode on a cherub, and flew,
> he came swiftly upon the wings of the wind.
>
> (Psalm 18:10–11)

He likewise envelops himself in darkness, throws down hailstones
and coals of fire, thunders and shoots forth lightnings (Psalm 18:12–
15). We cross a threshold to find ourselves in a strange reality, where
we can assume neither that the smoke and lava of a volcanic eruption
emerge from the nostrils and the mouth of God (verse 9), nor that
all these images are anything more than a hyperbolic account of the
victory of God over the enemies of David. I think of the moment in
the second book of Kings where Elisha prays to God to open the eyes
of his servant, and the young man suddenly sees what Elisha was
already seeing, that the mountain is "full of horses and chariots of
fire"—full of a heavenly army (2 Kings 6:17). The psalmist similarly
sees something; he no doubt sees, thanks to his imagination, the real,
where the visible and invisible worlds interpenetrate, where the phys-
ical universe is found mingled with the spiritual universe, where the
earth is filled with heaven.

All the poetry of the Psalms leads us to look upon the world
otherwise. To see solitude: "I am like a lonely bird on the housetop"
(Psalm 102:8); to see enemies: "Their mouth is an open sepulcher"
(5:10); to see the immensity of the real: "Out of the depths I cry to
thee, O LORD!" (130:1), "O God . . . from the end of the earth I call
to thee" (61:3). We pass, in Psalm 139, from ordinary and customary
details of the here and now—about which the poet already is filled
with wonder, recognizing that God knows when he sits and when he
rises, when he walks and when he lies down, that he foresees everything

he thinks and says and that he surrounds him with his presence—to sudden flights into the extraordinary. Where would I go, he asks him, to flee from you?

> If I ascend to heaven, you are there,
> if I make my bed in Sheol, you are there.
> If I take the wings of dawn,
> or dwell in the uttermost parts of the sea,
> even there your hand shall lead me,
> and your right hand shall hold me.
> If I say, Surely the darkness shall cover me,
> even the night shall be light about me.
>   (Psalm 139:8–11)

The Psalms open the real to us, they change our way of perceiving it, not according to the personal vision of the poets, but according to their faith: they transform the world into itself, into a living work of God, vibrating with his presence. The poets' imagination allows them, in relation to their religion, to respond to the invitation of God, addressed to Adam, addressed to man, to name creation, to modify it by welcoming it into human consciousness and language.

I will risk an interpretation of the parallelism that is so characteristic of Hebrew poetry. The synthetic parallelism in Psalm 19:8–9:

> The law of the LORD is perfect, reviving the soul,
> the testimony of the LORD is sure, making wise the simple,
> the precepts of the LORD are right, rejoicing the heart,
> the commandments of the LORD are luminous,
>   enlightening the eyes

corresponds to the very first commandment in Genesis to be fruitful and multiply, and recalls the exuberance of the world at its origin. The antithetical parallelism, "For the wicked shall be cut off, / but those who wait for the LORD shall possess the land" (Psalm 37:9), manifests the divided condition of a fallen world. The synonymic parallelism, as in Psalm 114:

> When Israel went forth from Egypt,
> the house of Jacob from a people of strange language,
> Judah became his sanctuary,
> Israel his dominion.
> The sea looked and fled,
> Jordan turned back,
> the mountains skipped like rams,
> the hills like lambs

constitutes, through its incessant variations, a repetition that is not disquieting but instead innovative. Through its joyful form, productive of the other within the same, it foresees the re-creation of all things in the "new heavens" and the "new earth."

6.

From the point of view of poetics in general, the Psalms thus offer an interesting perspective on the great and thorny question of translation. They explain the unexpected power of words, the creative virtue of language, by addressing speech to a God whose voice, which formed the universe, continues to exercise its power. They display the essential relationship between poetry and praise. They shine light on the mystery of what happens to the self of the poet in the act of writing. The author of Psalm 81, in affirming, "I hear a tongue I had not known," anticipates the moment in "Little Gidding," the last of T. S. Eliot's *Four Quartets*, where the "I" who speaks, already a figure wrought and distanced from the poet, declares: "I . . . cried / And heard another's voice cry." The Psalms give access above all to a certain way of seeing the real, where what we now call imagination grasps the presence around us, and sometimes even the appearing, of another world.

From the Christian point of view, they illuminate the way in which it is given to us to speak of God, and of the world in relation to him. They do more than express faith: they incarnate it, in the verbalized and shaped experience of a concrete individual, who opens his most secret places. Through confession, supplication, thanksgiving, and praise the psalmists tend toward God—without the encumbrance of argument, without believing themselves obliged either to doubt or to persuade themselves first of all that he exists. Sometimes in the movement of their writings, as sudden joy invades a psalm of distress, they show *change*, this reversal of the sign, the death and resurrection found at the heart of life. Psalm 22, which begins, "My God, my God, why have you abandoned me?" ends with the conversion of all the nations of the world. In Psalm 13, we pass from another feeling of abandonment: "How long, O LORD? Will you forget me forever?" to "the LORD... has dealt bountifully with me." (The silence heard in the course of each of these poems, tying distress to joy, constitutes a secret, wordless place that invites our meditation.) Faith in the Psalms is not presented as a collection of beliefs. The psalmists implore, praise, and thank a God who is Presence, who listens, who forgives, and who is first and foremost the Creator of a work that is marvelous, unfolding in history as much as in the heavens and the earth, day and night, the seasons and the weather. This wonder is not simply aesthetic; the author of Psalm 18, whose God covers himself in darkness and rides on a cherub, begins: "I love you, O LORD." Love nourishes the wonder, which nourishes the love.

Cries, stories, images. A *vocative* poetry that is addressed to God and to his creation. The Psalms remind us that the entire Bible proceeds in this way, that the New Testament offers not a methodical exposition of the truth, but consists of a series of brief biographies—in which Jesus also constantly tells stories—a short narration of the life of the first Christians, a collection of letters and a figurative and visionary book. The Psalms remind us that the Judeo-Christian religion, systematized by European thought, has as its matrix a Middle Eastern culture with its own ways of proceeding. If we are tempted to read the end of Psalm 85 as a poem from the personification-loving eighteenth century, where love and truth meet and justice and peace kiss (85:11), we suddenly come upon this: "Truth will spring from the earth." Our way of seeing is disrupted by this refusal of abstraction, or rather, by its absence, by a realism that challenges what we are used to. A truth that springs from the earth assumes, in a way that I do not claim to understand, that reality *is* metaphorical, and that it is thanks to poetry, to the imagination, that life, faith, and love grasp the truth, which has its dwelling place, so to speak, in the real. It leads us to Jesus's declaration, which is even more mysterious, deeply poetic, and absolutely revolutionary: "I am … the truth."

POETRY AND ISAIAH'S BURNING COAL

I.

POETRY sheds light on the Bible; but what does the Bible say about poetry? What is poetry from the biblical point of view? The question could turn out to be dangerous. About poetry, the Bible says nothing explicitly; we must extrapolate, at the risk of making our desires speak rather than the biblical writings. The scriptures are presented as a library of books having as their aim "teaching, reproof, correction, and training in righteousness" (2 Timothy 3:16); this should not be forgotten, nor should we make a chancy amalgam of theology and poetics. Nevertheless, the Bible has very close relations with poetry, and the fact that so many of its books are written in poetry requires reflection. As I've said, the poetry in the book of Job, or in the books of the prophets, is not added to the text as an embellishment, or in order to make the "message" more memorable, or for the writer's pleasure. What the text expresses is difficult to separate from an increase of significance born of poetic form, with its transformed syntax, its both meaningful and musical placement of words, its foregrounding of sound and rhythm. The message of salvation comes in the mind and the body of poetic speech; message and poetry arrive together. An appropriate and complete reading of Jeremiah, for instance, would proceed according to what we would call in other circumstances literary criticism, and this would likewise be the case for the biblical works in prose, where the act of writing is no less evident. (This is not to say that literary critics are uniquely capable of understanding the Bible, as once it was claimed that only phi-

POETRY AND ISAIAH'S BURNING COAL · 89

lologists were competent to understand literature; nor am I claiming that the present infatuation with the "literary" study of the Bible is a great step forward: more often than not its dilettantism misses the essential.) One may thus regret that theologians, considering the texts from a certain perspective in a way similar to the philosopher who seeks to grasp what Spinoza or Hegel meant and in what contexts they wrote, are unprepared to pay heed to what is composed and written.

The brief but charged sixth chapter of Isaiah exemplifies the Bible's poetics. At once radical and liminal, the chapter is set apart from the chapters that surround it. It tells of Isaiah's vocation, and of course we need not imagine that every poet would find himself called in such a manner. The word that the prophet must speak concerns the rejection of God and the salvation that is nevertheless being prepared; in studying the poetics that emerges from the chapter we should remember that it is only an epiphenomenon in relation to the book's primordial concerns. Nevertheless, Isaiah is engaged consciously in an act of writing, of poetry. An adequate response to his words must be religious, existential, and poetic. Isaiah is totally invested in his poem; by trying to perceive *all* the lessons that Isaiah seems to propose, the reader can likewise invest himself in the act of reading.

Here is the well-known first part of this instructive short work:

> In the year that King Uzziah died I saw the Lord sitting
>   upon a throne, high and lifted up, and his train filled
>   the temple.
> Above him stood the seraphim; each had six wings: with
>   two he covered his face, and with two he covered his
>   feet, and with two he flew.
> One called to another and said:
> Holy, holy, holy is the LORD of hosts,
> the whole earth is full of his glory.
>
> The threshold in its foundations shook at the voice of him
>   who called, and the house was filled with smoke. And I said:

Woe is me! For I am lost;
for I am a man of unclean lips,
and I dwell in the midst of a people of unclean lips;
for my eyes have seen the King, the LORD of hosts!

Then flew one of the seraphim to me, having in his hand a
burning coal which he had taken with tongs from the altar.
He touched my mouth, and said:

Behold, this has touched your lips,
your guilt is taken away,
your sin forgiven.

One senses that each detail counts, and that the allusion to the
death of Uzziah is not just there to provide a date for the supernatu-
ral vision. The prophet receives his call in a world where men die, and
if one reads this chapter as an exemplary poem, the poet too begins,
under the sign of death, the most incontestable manifestation of the
sorrow of our condition. The poet who feels that poetry is born from
this strange punishment—from this punishment that creates the
strange—is well placed to pursue his task, to seek patiently, to over-
come sorrow, to discover the signs, in the world and in the self, of
something beyond the Fall. In the case of Isaiah, the vision of a beyond
arrives with the very mention of death, as if to insist on the immense
gulf between "the year that King Uzziah died" and "I saw the Lord."
Maybe poetry always begins with such a double awareness, of sorrow
but also of *something else*: not necessarily of God, and certainly not
in the precise way it does for Isaiah, yet with a presentiment of some
wondrous possibility within reality that it is poetry's task to deepen.
Faced with death, both poetry and our own well-being afford us a
glimpse of another light within the real, a vision that at the same
time directs us back to death, giving the vision its urgency.

The seraphim add to the inviting strangeness of the scene. Isaiah
describes them in detail, attending closely to their three pairs of wings;

they do not figure anywhere else in the Hebrew Bible. They too are poets, and it is a poem that Isaiah is listening to at the moment of his calling. The seraphim are immersed in their vision of God's inexhaustible holiness, a vision of the earth entirely filled with divine glory. Here we find another astonishing change of perspective: the earth is the place of our death and of all the sorrow that precedes it, but it is also and before all else the place of the radiant presence of God, which appears in a special and spectacular way for Isaiah, but which awaits a gaze capable of discerning it in every place and at every moment. God is present here and now, as he is everywhere and always. The beginning of inspiration for Isaiah, the beginning of the *work* of the poet, would be the vision, in the surrounding world, of a splendor that is at once natural and foreign. For the atheist poet, this would be the intuition of an increase of the real within ordinary reality. In listening to the seraphim sing the glory of God, Isaiah also learns that poetry begins in praise and culminates in praise, and that the most sublime vision is not meant for his personal use. The seraphim do not concern themselves with him but instead respond to one another (or from one choir to another), and they do not explore the depths of their own inner life.

The effect of their poetry is immediate and gripping: "And the posts of the door moved at the voice of him that cried." The sentence is difficult to translate, for (if I have understood correctly) the words for "posts" and "door" can also mean threshold and foundations, or even a doorstep and a threshold. The New Jerusalem Bible proposes "the door-posts," but the New English Bible translates: "The threshold shook to its foundations," and Claudel, in *L'Évangile d'Isaïe*, offers the "*fondements des seuils*," the foundations of the thresholds. In every case, poetry—and more particularly the *voice* of poetry— operates on the real. It makes it vibrate: it allows the gaze of being to see reality otherwise. As in the ever-accurate myth of Orpheus, whose sung poetry moves the trees and slows the course of rivers, the voice of the seraphim, also superhuman, disturbs the material world, the presences of our sojourn; it is a supernatural sign of the natural power of human poetry. If a threshold is meant, we perceive even more clearly the ability of poetry to open the world for us, to cross a trembling limit, to penetrate into the otherness of things.

But it is not with wonder alone that Isaiah is filled by a new vision of the world and of the power of poetry. He sees himself, above all, as guilty: "I am lost, / for I am a man of unclean lips, / and I dwell in the midst of a people of unclean lips." He does not react like Moses: "I am not gifted for speech" (Exodus 4:10), or Jeremiah: "I do not know how to speak" (Jeremiah 1:6). If he thinks of his mouth as "unclean lips," a figure that he alone uses in the Bible, it is because he perceives language as bearing the most disturbing and noxious expression of sin. (I think of "the tongue is an evil world" in the letter of James in the New Testament, 3:6.) As a sinner, he recognizes that his body and everything that comes out of his being is evil, and that the same evil extends to all those who surround him: the sudden vision of heaven convinces him of the earth's woe. As a man, he knows himself incapable of the endlessly laudative *extraspection* of the seraphim; as a poet, he knows that his mouth is incapable of their poetic language, which is at once beautiful, good, and true. A poet coming from a totally different region of poetry can understand the importance and the creative opportuneness of this beginning in powerlessness and in self-distrust with regard to the supreme value of the real.

For Isaiah, the world is at the same time more glorious and more lamentable than for those who do not see it in the biblical perspective. And I cannot resist the temptation to note the similarity between this Hebrew poetry and English poetry. In a few verses, Isaiah passes from the heavens to the earth; from God and the seraphim to lips and eyes, to a door and then to tongs and a coal; from the shaking of doorposts to the idea of uncleanness. A vision of the transcendent is inseparable from the evocation of concrete objects and gestures, while another idea, that of death, circulates beneath it all. And what does the burning coal, which answers Isaiah's anguish by purifying his lips, mean for us? Isaiah is in the temple, near the altar where the holocaust is presented, the sacrifice consumed by fire, and we realize that as prophet,

the lips with which he will announce the divine word must be puri-
fied and that, more profoundly, the "iniquity" and the "sin" that make
them unclean must be wiped away. But as poet? Even the ordinary
poet, who has not seen God and who will not speak in his name, can
recognize that he is unfit for writing, and that in order to attain to
poetic speech, his entire being must change, so as to find a right rela-
tion with a reality seeking to be expressed that is greater than he. This
is not about the quest for pure poetry, nor those fine sentiments that
lead most often, as Gide was right to say, to mediocre literature. It is
about cleansing one's motivations, listening to rather than manipulat-
ing language, awaiting the coming poem, discerning one's own and
others' true aspirations, distinguishing the deep movement of the real.
Let us not forget either that while Isaiah witnesses a radiant splendor
before being purified, it is only after that he can write his vision.

2.

The vision in the sanctuary, the recognition of sin, and the purifica-
tion with the burning coal constitute for the prophet and the poet a
veritable *Urszene*, a primal scene, an originating theater that lies at
the beginning of his work, and to which he can constantly return.
Here is how the piece continues:

> And I heard the voice of the Lord saying:
>> Whom shall I send, and who will go for us?
> And I said: Here am I! Send me.
> And he said:
>> Go, and say to this people:
>> Hear and hear, but do not understand,
>> and see and see, but do not perceive.
>> Make the heart of this people fat,
>> and their ears heavy, and shut their eyes,
>> lest they see with their eyes,

and hear with their ears,
and understand with their hearts,
and turn and be healed.
Then I said: How long, O Lord?
And he said: Until cities lie waste without inhabitants, and houses without men, and the land is utterly desolate, and the LORD removes men far away, and the forsaken places are many in the midst of the land.

And though a tenth remain in it, it will be burned again, like a terebinth or an oak, whose stump remains standing when it is felled: the holy seed is its stump.

This is the moment to notice two things. Isaiah moves continually from prose to verse, with a precision, however, that is difficult to determine: in my own translation, I follow the schema of the New Jerusalem Bible, which corresponds fairly closely to the New English Bible. It seems that verse is reserved for the speech of the seraphim, of Isaiah, and of God, as if to underscore that poetry is first of all an oral art form, words that one pronounces and listens to, a language that leads toward the sounds of words, or toward words as sounds. But then Isaiah recalls that, while our language passes through unclean lips and participates in our woe, it is also allied with—but how to understand this?—the logos, the Word, the Word of a God who created the world by speaking it, by making a few immense words resonate in the abyss. By listening to this second lesson, of woe and happiness, one recognizes that the message of God—after the splendor of his presence, the canticle of the seraphim, and the glowing coal that purifies Isaiah to the depths—begins in the most complete misery, as the announcement of the destruction of the land and the spiritual deafness of the people. And yet this is a capital message, intended to warn the nation that it risks missing out on salvation: it is quoted by Jesus in each of the four Gospels (Matthew 13:14, Mark 4:12, Luke 8:10, John 12:39–40), and by Paul in the Acts of the Apostles (28:25–27). One might have expected that a poet, thus prepared, would dispense joy. But it is not over, for the last words of the chapter hold an even greater surprise. They are difficult to read, the Hebrew being, according to the specialists, rather obscure. And yet, wherever one sets the punctuation and whatever the presumed syntax, it seems reasonable to think that the remnant of the people of Israel, even though felled, will constitute a stump containing the seed of the future race. The entirety of the word that Isaiah must deliver is thus fundamental: it expresses the dynamic idea of the Old Testament, that there will be deafness and blindness, but that from a remnant there will be born a "holy" seed that will respond to the "holy" God of the seraphim's canticle. When in the light of poetry one meditates on this long-awaited good news, one can conclude that Isaiah advances as far into the heart of religion as that of poetry, and that once made clean he immediately discovers the essential. As a poem, his chapter six is admirably complete. It begins with death, passes through a vision that brings self-knowledge and the desire to be transformed, and speaks at length of the distress of mankind before coming to an end in a distant joy. The task of poetry would be to counter evil, to catch a glimpse of *something else*, and to act on reality, or the way in which we perceive it, just as the voice of the seraphim shakes the doorposts of our earthly home. With its repeated coming and going between prose and verse, this short piece of writing, so charged with material, continually draws us toward a speech beyond language and toward a way of being that surpasses ordinary existence. Through its form, it offers the ideal model for all poetry, by descending before climbing higher: the death of Uzziah is followed by the vision of God; the feeling of sinfulness by a purification of the whole being; the anticipation of a rebel people and a ravaged land by the obscure and thus all the more precious promise of a barely comprehensible holy seed. By advancing from death, and from the vision of another dimension in the real, toward this promise that withdraws into the future, it situates poetry in the long *between time* that we are all living, which extends from loss to salvation. It even confirms classicism and romanticism considered, outside history, as two viewpoints on the nature of poetry, through its economy and its rigorous and complex structure, and through its visionary, strange, and innovative orientation. If the only poem remaining were chapter 6 of Isaiah, we would have a very rich and elevated idea of poetry.

And that is not all, for poetic writing is strongly present in this piece. From where, suddenly, do the terebinth and the oak come? They do not seem to serve merely to make a proposition clearer, to explain that the people, even decimated, will maintain the hope of being reborn just as certain trees, cruelly cut back, still remain living. The comparison is not the invention of a reasoning poet, it is revelatory: the link between the two entities exists in reality, nature dies and is reborn, the people of God likewise. Another comparison arises almost immediately, at the beginning of chapter seven; the juxtaposition is striking, whether it results from Isaiah's decision or that of an editor. It is announced to the king of Judah that an enemy is approaching, "and his heart and the heart of his people shook as the trees of the forest shake before the wind" (Isaiah 7:2). Men once again resemble trees, and we sense that the wind in the forest is not mentioned solely to show how much the inhabitants of Jerusalem are troubled. A singular and intimate relation is created between men and these other upright beings, the trees; the powerful wind, the invisible breath that manifests itself, seems—thanks to the poetry, to the comparison through which it slips into the reader's mind—almost numinous. When we discover that in the text the wind is *ruah*, we find ourselves in the primitive land of true poetry. We are accustomed to saying that *ruah*, *pneuma* in Greek and *spiritus* in Latin, mean at the same time, and curiously, *wind*, *breath*, and *spirit*, assuming with Max Müller in *The Science of Language* that the material meanings, *wind* and *breath*, gave birth, at the moment when someone saw the possibility of making a metaphor, to the spiritual meaning, to the idea of a spirit that would be the principle of life. However, we must *listen* to these words, and be attentive above all to what Jesus says in chapter 3 of the Gospel of John. He teaches Nicodemus that one must be born of pneuma, and that, as "the pneuma blows where it wills, and you hear the sound of it, but you do not know whence it comes or whither it goes," so it is "with everyone who is born of the pneuma" (John 3:8). In translating, we pass from *Spirit* to *wind* and once again to *Spirit*, without being able to measure the strangeness of this profoundly poetic language, and without thinking, as Owen Barfield already proposed in 1928 in his *Poetic Diction*, that instead of progressively aggregating a series of different meanings, such words must have had a single meaning at their origin, which we labor to grasp, before the distinctions between material and spiritual, literal and figurative, were invented. Perhaps we catch a glimpse of this primitive meaning at the very beginning of the Bible, which declares that "the ruah of God was moving over the face of the waters."

Through these two comparisons Isaiah transports us upstream from our categories, into a world where the real changes, where men and trees share birth and rebirth and feel the same mysterious breath upon them. Our wonder grows when we reflect that the domain of poetry is quite precisely the ruah—to employ our split vocabulary: poetry is carried by breath, it resonates in the air and speaks to our spirit—and when we notice that hearts and trees are *moved* exactly as the posts of the door are *moved*, according to the same Hebrew verb. The voice of the seraphim, a worrisome piece of news, and the wind in the forest act in some way in concert. We enter into contact here with the joy of writing in these comparisons that give onto a primitive unity, as well as in the form of the verses and their parallelism. This joy of the reader and of the writer represents another way of standing up against evil, of distinguishing a hope beyond what is said, beyond the desperate feeling of sin, of distress to come, or of the enemy's approach. An irresistible joy doubtless constitutes the fundamental principle of writing, which explains why the books of the Bible, which do not belong solely to what we now call literature, but which have vital teachings to deliver and to make understood, always probe language deeply, in its resources and the forms that it calls forth.

3.

One could also consider the beauty of the writing, and develop the reflections on beauty that this apparent luxury inspires. Why is biblical poetry beautiful? What is beauty in the light of the Bible? What are its origin and its end? It is once again the beauty of the disagreeable that is the most instructive. Since at least Aristotle it is affirmed that the imitation of what displeases us is pleasant, but we also know that the beauty of language, like that of painting or of music, redeems the displeasing by opening it to what surpasses it, and that the beauty of the work and the beauty that the work allows us to discern create at the same time the conviction that there exists a world that escapes us, and the imperative desire to go there. Whence the joy and the sadness of all beauty, and the ambiguous tears that it causes to flow. And shouldn't we add that beauty is infinite? The beauty of a work, and that of the world. The infinite beauty of the finite is wonder-inducing, paradoxical, mysterious. In an object, a being, a landscape, in the whole universe, it gives us the premonition of an absence of limits and another way of being. Undeniably, it gives onto a beyond. When the seraphim declare before Isaiah that the whole earth is full of the glory of God, we barely understand, even if we believe in God, and the reason lies in our incapacity *to see*. But beauty offers us, if only from time to time, a fugitive glimpse of the special splendor that inhabits, sustains, and surrounds all that is. Wordsworth called beauty "a living Presence of the earth": his poet's clairvoyance and his human sensibility allowed him to appreciate how beauty lives and how it belongs to the being of the real, setting aside the sterile definitions of beauty that Europeans seem to be led to seek out because of a certain turn of mind. Beauty is also the infinite presence of the earth, the dimension of our earthly sojourn that can persuade us that death, albeit omnipresent, does not reign.

If beauty is infinite, it already participates in the sublime, and it is normal that it perplexes us. In a world fallen, or miserable for any other reason, beauty appears incompatible with the suffering of people and the untiring work of evil. And indeed it is: it speaks of a world that is gone, and of a world to come. The earth is finite, and its infinite beauty constitutes the most palpable sign of the re-creation of our temporary home, of the "new earth" that is to come. Or should we say, not *infinite*—for we have no conception at all of the infinite and magically produce the contrary of what we know by adding to the word *finite* a negative prefix—but the other-than-finite, a condition of time and space that exceeds what we experience? And note that beauty is not an unfixed entity dissociable from what is beautiful: the beauty of the earth is inseparable from the earth, it is beautiful earth, other-than-finite, that will continue under a different form, just as the human body will continue. Note above all that beauty is the only other-than-finite thing that strikes the senses. Perhaps we are certain that love, or truth, or justice surpass our finitude, but only beauty puts our senses, our body, in contact with another state of being, with what lies beyond our material universe, whether it is the beauty of the earth, of a person, a drawing, a sculpture, a piece of music, a narration, or this poem by Isaiah. Beauty suggests, to our eyes, to our ears, to the rhythm of our body, the existence of a greater reality; it attracts our body, and our spirit, toward the wide open.

Beauty at once sensible and (as it were) infinite helps us to grasp better a fundamental but difficult passage in the first letter to the Corinthians. Paul affirms there that just as a kernel of grain by dying becomes a plant that in appearance is completely different, so a man is sown "a natural body" and is raised "a spiritual body" (15:44). The oxymoron of the spiritual body also establishes a relation between the corporal and the infinite, and while Paul does not evoke beauty, he does speak of the *doxa*, of the glory that the seraphim of Isaiah saw everywhere on the earth. The celestial bodies have their own glory, he writes, just like the terrestrial bodies of men, beasts, fish, and birds; the sun's glory differs from that of the moon, and that of the stars, and each star has its own particular glory. In death one is sown in "dishonor," one rises "in glory" (15:43)—in another sort of glory, of which the glory of the sun, for example, its radiance, its beauty, is already the visible sign that is plain to see.

Poetry, from the biblical point of view, aspires to a beauty that gives a premonition of the nonfinite, and which hints at change. In theology, change is at the heart of Paul's declaration to the Corinthians, "We shall all be changed" (1 Corinthians 15:51), and to the Philippians, "Christ...will change our lowly bodies to be like his glorious body" (Philippians 3:21). In poetry, writing transfigures, if not the real (like the voice of the seraphim that shakes the doorposts), then at least our vision of the real, when an alarming piece of news acts on the human heart like the wind in the forest on the trees' branches. Beauty, finally (but there is no end to these sorts of reflections, and the chapter from Isaiah remains inexhaustible), beauty, by its simple appearance and whatever may be the horror that it covers, is so far in excess in relation to the rest, it transcends our expectation and our capacity to such an extent that it opens onto the future, with the promise that all shall be well.

THE MOST BEAUTIFUL OF SONGS

I.

WE UNDERSTAND that the Bible is foreign to us when we discover the Song of Songs, with its astonishing poetry, so extravagant and properly Middle Eastern. How should one read such a work, and speak of it? From the beginning to the end, it is about the exalted love between a man and a woman, and in order to convert all this ardent sensuality into discourse about God, into spiritual revelation, the Jewish and Christian traditions have proposed an allegorical reading. Since, however, there exists in the entire poem only a single allusion to God, many commentators, starting with Herder and Goethe, set aside the religious interpretations by privileging the play of the lovers and the play of the poetry. They assume that the Song sings of the pleasure, the ecstasy of a purely human love, without any sacred dimension, thanks to a poetic art that itself enters into ecstasy, and the pleasure of which lies in creating a complete harmony between the lovers and a nature that is likewise purely natural. If they are right to restrain the poem in this way, it is doubtless necessary to question its inclusion among the scriptures. If they are wrong, their very understandable mistrust of an allegorical reading should encourage us to seek another way to read the poem, while keeping in mind its undeniable hinterland of allusions. Above all, we should ask if at the heart of the Song's poetry one can discern a spacious meaning that, while going beyond the being and the consciousness of the lovers, does not involve allegory.

The work's title, the Song of Songs, follows the form of the superlative in Hebrew and signifies the song par excellence, the most beautiful of songs. It draws attention to the existence of the work as a poem, the essential of what it achieves being found, indeed, in its title. The Song is above all a work of poetry, a sort of cantata for three voices in which the poet concentrates without interruption not on the God of Israel and the fate of the nation, but on a love story, exercising his art with a joyful exuberance. But the title seems to declare at the same time that, as the exemplary song—*the* song—the Song deals with fundamental things. How is this possible?

2.

Let us think first about the allusions in the text, which seem to give an allegorical exegesis its purchase. The confident chant of the young woman, "My beloved is mine and I am his" (Song of Songs 2:16), which she takes pleasure in repeating in reverse order, "I am my beloved's and my beloved is mine" (6:3), as if to weave together more solidly their mutual belonging—this radiant chant recalls the formula of the covenant between God and Israel: "I will take you for my people, and I will be your God" (Exodus 6:7). When she becomes, for the young man, the "bride" (in the very middle of the poem, between Song of Songs 4:8 and 5:1), it may be remembered that God is presented as the bridegroom of Israel, and that the prophet Isaiah expresses his emotion before this signal election in the following way:

> I greatly rejoice in the LORD,
> my soul exults in my God,
> for he has clothed me with the garments of salvation,
> he has covered me with a robe of righteousness,
> as a bridegroom decks himself with a garland,
> and as a bride adorns herself with her jewels.
>
> (Isaiah 61:10)

And yet, the covenant and the marriage of God with Israel appear only momentarily, in the space of one verse or a few, and the foreground of the poem contains too many details foreign to this covenant and marriage for us to be constantly conscious of it. If we remain convinced that the poem speaks of something other than the love of the two beloveds, we have to give up on what we ordinarily call an allegorical reading and accept that the poem allows it to be glimpsed only in certain moments charged with emotion and thought.

The poem's allowance for a movement beyond human love can guide us in all our exegeses. As when we discern another "allegory" that really is not one: the love of Jesus and of the Christian. We know well enough that most of the things that the lovers say to each other, with the passion that motivates them, would not be said between Jesus and us. The only moment, I believe, where a Christian would see that the text speaks with his voice takes place once again in the young woman's refrain: "My beloved is mine and I am his" (Song of Songs 2:16). But that does not forbid us from thinking that the love of the man for the woman, whom he sees as "perfect" (5:2, 6:9), must be like that of God for us, who sees us as we ought to be, as we are in Jesus, and as we shall be, according to the promise, in the new world. Nor are we forbidden to note that the beloved, both serene and anxious, resembles us. Nor to convince ourselves that the inflamed and complete concentration of the lovers on their love and on one another reveals what ought to be our love for God. However, whether such reflections belong to the poem or come from the reader, we are once again dealing with suggestions on the text's horizon.

Another "allegory," the love of God for Jerusalem, puts us on the path of a better reading of the work. The unique status of the beloved, "the fairest among women" (5:9) for whom the lover will make "pendants of gold / and beads of silver" (1:11), evokes the city of Jerusalem in the prophecy of Ezekiel, "decked with gold and silver" by the attentions of Yahweh and "more and more beautiful [and] renowned among the nations for [her] beauty" (Ezekiel 16:13–14). With Jerusalem, however, the story continues. God accuses her of "serving as a prostitute" (16:15) and of having committed countless abominations, and declares that she will be punished. But everything changes when, suddenly, the future opens: "Yet I will remember," God tells her, "my covenant with you in the days of your youth, and I will establish with you an everlasting covenant.... I will forgive you all that you have done" (16:60–63). Ezekiel catches only a fleeting glimpse of this future of newness and forgiveness, and if all of this seems to be distant from the Song of Songs, it is enough to look to the end of the book of Revelation. "I saw," writes John, "the holy city, new Jerusalem, coming down out of heaven from God, prepared as a bride adorned for her husband" (Revelation 21:2). Might we think that the author of the Song, when creating the perfect beauty of the beloved, had in mind at the same time the Jerusalem that he knew and the possible radiant future of the holy city? He does not have the benefit of Isaiah's vision—"As a young man marries a virgin, / your builder shall marry you. / And as the bridegroom rejoices over the bride, / so shall your God rejoice over you" (Isaiah 62:5)—but his poem allows the discernment, from afar, of these nuptials of the end of time.

For us, the New Jerusalem represents in part the Church, and according to the Christian allegorical reading, the love of God and of the Church is prefigured in the love of the two beloveds. When we read numerous texts of the New Testament, the astonishment and enchantment of the lovers in the Song of Songs indeed come to mind. Once again, for example, the book of Revelation: "Then came one of the seven angels ... and spoke to me, saying, 'Come, I will show you the Bride, the wife of the Lamb.' And in the Spirit he carried me away to a great, high mountain, and showed me the holy city Jerusalem" (21:9–10); "Let us rejoice and exult and give him the glory, for the marriage of the Lamb has come, and his Bride has made herself ready" (19:7). Paul addresses himself thus to the Christians of Corinth: "I feel a divine jealousy for you, for I betrothed you to one husband, as a chaste virgin to Christ" (2 Corinthians 11:2). When the same Paul declares to the Ephesians, in the midst of his discourse on the duty of husbands and wives, that Christ gave himself up for the Church, "for he wanted to present the church to himself in splendor, without spot or wrinkle or any such thing, that she might be holy and without blemish" (Ephesians 5:27), we recognize the beloved of the Song, "without spot" (Song 4:7) and "perfect" (6:9). There also exists a possible link between the formula used by John in the book of Revelation when he evokes the marriage of the Lamb with his spouse, "Let us rejoice and exult" (19:7), and the cry of joy of the beloved at the beginning of the Song of Songs: "Let us exult and rejoice in you" (1:4). It is true that the words do indeed constitute a formula that is often employed in the Old Testament and taken up by the Gospel according to Matthew at the end of the Beatitudes (5:12). Nevertheless, it may be that the cry of the beloved, as conventional as it is enthusiastic, to the "king" of her heart culminates (like the expression itself) in the apocalyptic cry of the "great multitude" that hails the Lamb and his bride. And yet, this presence of the Church in the Song is ghostly. We cannot read the poem while thinking of the Church in each instant, and, like every allegory in the Old Testament (which announces an evangelical truth without the author being fully aware of it), the love of the two beloveds offers only a glimpse of the ultimate direction of history and of the ultimate meaning of the poem.

3.

The same can be said regarding a hidden meaning, already illuminated by the commentators. It relies on a prolonged play on words, which appears from the very beginning of the poem. The first five verses introduce the words *shelomo* ("Solomon"), then *shemen* ("oil") and *shem* ("name"), in the sentence, "Your name is oil poured out," and finally *yerushalem* ("Jerusalem"). These sounds that recur and that are born from the poet's pleasure, from the making evident in poetry of the language's sonorities in view of creating an audible beauty and suggesting new relations in the real—these sounds draw attention to the name of Solomon and names in general, and to the *peace* (*shalom*) that is heard in "Solomon" and "Jerusalem." Indeed, "Solomon" means "the peaceful." At the end of the poem, the beloved is called the "Shulammite" (Song 7:1); the word may be a feminine form of *Solomon* and may signify "the pacified." Just before the poem ends, she affirms having found "in his eyes . . . peace" (*shalom*, 8:10). The play on words having begun at the beginning as a sort of throw of the dice, in the end finds its reason for being, its completion, in the peace that finally emerges, and that declares the deep relationship between the man and the woman. The couple, anonymous but clothed by the poem with the names of Solomon and the Shulammite, the peaceful and the pacified, manifests in their union this peace that the Old Testament seeks and foresees and that the New Testament reveals. Among the numerous expressions of a desire for spiritual peace, Psalm 122 plays on the name of Jerusalem in order to make of the city the seemingly predestined dwelling place of peace: "For the peace of Jerusalem pray: / May those who love you be peaceful! / May peace be within your ramparts: / may your palaces be peaceful!" (6–7). In Isaiah's vision, the child who will sit on the throne of David will be called "Prince of Peace" (Isaiah 9:6), and the man of sorrows upon whom God lays our faults, through his chastisement "gives us peace" (Isaiah 53:5). At the birth of Jesus, the angels sang, "Glory to God in the highest / and on earth peace among men with whom he is pleased" (Luke 2:14); once the work of Jesus is accomplished, God himself becomes "the God of peace" (e.g., Romans 15:33). It is as if—at the end of the poem where certain words retroactively shed light on all that we have read—the immense connotations of the word *peace*, the reconciliation and harmony of all things under the sun and beyond, were emerging in the love of the two lovers. Or rather, these connotations could be perceived in the distance, as the final goal and meaning of a poem that we have just read in a different perspective: by interesting ourselves in a love story, in the absence of peace for the woman, who sometimes seeks her lover without finding him and who declares herself "sick with love" (Song 5:8), and for the man, who asks the woman to turn her eyes away, "for they disturb me" (6:5). We sense in the poem a future of which the lovers are not conscious, and that the poet barely understands. It is through poetry, through an arrangement at once ludic and serious of the words (a process in which prose, too, finds its pleasure and its gravity, but that poetic compactness and orality especially favor) that the author creates the latent and, so to speak, future meaning of his poem.

4.

The lovers, anonymous but charged with reality and even an individuality more marked than that of many fictive lovers whose inner life is revealed to us, make us sense what is beyond them. Above all they allow a new way of seeing nature—or better, despite the near absence of God, of seeing creation. The commentators have indeed seen that the allusion the man makes to "honey" and to "milk" found under the woman's tongue (Song 4:11) refers to the emblematic image of the promised land, so frequent in the Pentateuch and the prophets: a land "flowing with milk and honey" (e.g., Exodus 3:8). A particular description of this blessed land seems to announce the abundant nature in which the lovers live: "For the LORD your God is bringing you into a good land, a land of brooks of water, of fountains and springs, flowing forth in valleys and hills, a land of wheat and barley, of vines and fig trees and pomegranates, a land of olive trees and honey" (Deuteronomy 8:7–9). However, the world of the lovers is improbably lush and varied; abundant, for example, in plants that normally do not grow together. We are in the realm of fiction, in a land that, if it recalls the promised land, seems to be even richer, and to represent an even more stirring promise.

We contemplate the world in which the lovers move thanks to their love. When they look at each other, often naked or imagined in that state, their eyes do not stop in order to lasciviously detail the body's charms, for they see, beyond the beloved person, and in him or her, the attractiveness, the life, and the variety of the world. Their gaze, filled with wonder, becomes clairvoyant, their love an inflamed means to perceive the real. It makes them sensitive, with more acuity and in a new way, to the beauty—to the reality—of a gazelle bounding over the hills (Song 2:8–9), of a flock of goats flowing like hair on the slopes of Mount Gilead (4:1). (Just as the love of God makes us more and more sensitive to beauty as a gift in a simple plum tree heavy with fruit, or a light at the sound of a small brook.) Their praise of the other makes them apt to see and praise everything around them.

They live poetically, opening themselves to the possible in each instant, to the poetry that changes the real, that makes the beloved a "dove hidden in the clefts of the rock" (Song 2:14) and the lover an apple tree in the "desired shadow" of which the beloved imagines herself seated (2:3). It is poetry that gives them access to this world in transformation, metaphors and comparisons that allow them to express the love that they feel for one another and their love of the earth, by constantly working the real. The metaphors and comparisons, as surprising as they might appear, are far from being embellishments; they participate in the lovers' vision and the meaning of the poem. The lovers see in each other, or with each other, the totality of creation. In what would be for us blazons of feminine and masculine bodies, there appear stones, metals, flowers, aromatic plants, trees, fruits, animals, birds, watercourses, mountains, cities, the heavens. The woman seems to reunite in her person, through the vision that she elicits in the man, the whole of the universe. She is associated with the earth, with its geography (Mounts Carmel, Gilead, Amana, Senir, Hermon) and its cities (Jerusalem, Tirzah, Sharon, Heshbon); she is beautiful "like the moon," resplendent "like the sun," imposing "like the starry sky" (Song 6:10; the meaning of these last words is uncertain). She is the world that returns after the darkness, she "comes forth like the dawn" (6:10).

Considering her in this way changes her by making of her a feminine and eminently lovable form of the world, which she also changes through the new perception that we gain of it. The woman likewise transports us to Genesis, toward the Creation, to the moment when God "made the two great lights, the greater one to govern the day, and the lesser one to govern the night; and he made the stars" (Genesis 1:16). The two beloveds, in the midst of a nature that is prolific, diverse, and capable of satisfying all the senses, resemble the man and woman of Genesis among the perfections of the original world. Would the poem then be the dream of an impossible return to Eden?

Even so, if the Song of Songs omits sin, it does bear the signs of the Fall. The violence suggested by the region that the bride comes from, the haunt of lions and panthers (Song 4:8), shows itself when the watchmen strike and wound her (5:7). The bride searches for her lover two times, worried at not finding him. Above all, it seems that the poem alludes three times to the moment when Adam and Eve begin to undergo the effects of their disobedience. What, deep down, do these words of the bride really mean?

> My beloved is mine, and I am his,
> he feeds among the lilies.
> Before the day-breeze rises
> and the shadows flee,
> return, my beloved, be like a gazelle,
> or a young stag
> upon rugged mountains.
>
> (Song 2:16–17)

"The day-breeze" recalls the fear of Adam and Eve after they have eaten the fruit, when they hear the footsteps of God walking in the garden "in the day-breeze" (Genesis 3:8), and they hide. However, while Adam and Eve also hide themselves from each other, recognizing their nakedness, the bride sings the joy of the love she shares with the beloved and invites him to return to her with the grace and the speed of a gazelle. The poet introduces this evocation of the first woe not in order to suggest that the lovers in his poem have recovered the condition of Adam and Eve before their act of disobedience, but to suggest that they live in a world where they almost do not suffer the consequences, where the day-breeze becomes simply the evening wind, cooling after the heat. The evocation returns:

> Before the day-breeze rises
> and the shadows flee,
> I shall go to the mountain of myrrh,
> to the hill of frankincense.
>
> (Song 4:6)

Once again, the context transforms the anxiety of Genesis into joyfulness. The beloved has just described the many beauties of the young woman; he continues, "You are all fair, my love, / without any flaw" (4:7). The other allusion to Genesis produces the same effect. The third time the young woman sings, "I belong to my beloved," she adds, "his yearning is for me" (7:11). The very rare word translated by "yearning" designates in Genesis the yearning of Eve, and of woman in general as figured by her, which shall be for her husband (Genesis 3:16). This desire for an Adam who "shall rule" over her is part of the punishment that God inflicts on her, while the yearning in the Song of Songs is joyful, and the poet, in transferring the yearning to the beloved, reconstitutes man and woman in a warmhearted reciprocity.

The Song of Songs does not envisage an Eden happily preserved from the Fall but rather a new world beyond the one that we know. This imagined world seems to culminate in certain powerful verses at the end, where the poem's tone is deepened and the voice of the bride becomes almost impersonal:

> Set me as a seal upon your heart,
> as a seal upon your arm.
> For love is strong as Death,
> jealousy unbending like the Grave.
> Its flames are flames of fire,
> a flame of the LORD.

(Song 8:6)

One might suppose several meanings for this passage. We can no more resist love than death. The strength of love is such that we brave death in its service. Jealousy is as demanding, or as cruel, as the grave. But perhaps the passage also recalls the punishment of the first human beings, in order to abolish it. The only love capable of resisting the death that struck Adam and his descendants because of his presumption is the love of God. The only jealousy that rules over the dwelling place of the dead is God's jealous love. And so it is that the flames of love come, indeed, from the Lord. In inducing the bride to reflect with passion, for the first time in the poem, on the very nature of love, the poet gives her—or creates for himself—this powerful

image of a condition beyond our own, where death, the final conse-
quence of the Fall, encounters the "consuming fire" of God (Deuter-
onomy 4:24), a passionate divine love that stands up to it.

5.

Is not this the vision, or rather the glimpse, at the heart of the Song
of Songs, of the faraway land that God revealed to Isaiah when he
said, "I am creating new heavens and a new earth" (Isaiah 65:17)?
While Isaiah, like Peter (2 Peter 3:13) and John (Revelation 21:1) who
quote him, speaks of the new Creation without describing this trans-
figured and indeed unimaginable earth, the poet of the Song suggests
it with the only means available to him (and available to every Chris-
tian poet), with the earth that he knows and that he presents under
the sign of a prodigious fullness. He constantly evokes not only a
world that is agreeable to the sight but, in a relatively short poem, an
intense concentration of flavors and scents: wine, honey, milk, raisin
cakes, pomegranate juice, fruit sweet on the palate; nard, myrrh,
henna, frankincense, saffron, calamus, cinnamon, aloes, balm, beds
of spices, banks sweetly scented, fragrance of Lebanon, "every exotic
perfume" (Song 3:6). To imagine such an exhilaration of scents and
flavors, to highlight the senses through which the exterior world
penetrates our bodies, allows him to modify this world in our think-
ing, thus suggesting its unusual richness.

This new world is a garden, incarnated in the bride. In this enclosed
garden there is a grove of pomegranate trees "with fruits of choicest
yield" (4:13), an imaginary gathering of innumerable and "choicest"
fragrances (4:14), and a "well of living water" (4:15). The poet recalls
the garden of Eden, planted with "every tree that is pleasant to the
sight and good for food" (Genesis 2:9) and watered with a river, but
he looks once again, not toward the past but toward the future. If the
bride is a garden, she invites the beloved there: "Let my lover come
to his garden, / and eat its fruits of choicest yield" (Song 4:16), and he
responds to the invitation: "I have come to my garden ... I eat my

honeycomb and my honey, / I drink my wine and my milk" (5:1). When they are thus making love, and a voice (that of the poet, or of the daughters of Jerusalem) urges them to rejoice in one another: "Eat, friends, drink, / drink deeply, lovers" (5:1), might we not imagine them in a new garden, where there is no more forbidden fruit and one at last eats the fruit of the tree of life (Genesis 3:22)?

On this new earth, a necessarily inadequate yet persuasive image of the true "new earth," nature abounds, flowers, and fills the air with fragrance more than our nature does, and gives only "the choice fruits," found "over our doors" (Song 7:14). Everything is improbable and marvelously exaggerated, and reminds us of what the angel will reveal to John in Revelation: "a tree of life, producing fruit twelve times a year, once each month" (Revelation 22:2). Everything, the lovers and all that surrounds them, is beautiful. While other poets of the Old Testament see in creation a multitude of creatures illuminated by the glory of God, and hear them continually singing out praise to the Creator, whether they be the sun, mountains, trees, animals, snow, or fog, the poet of the Song of Songs conceives of a nature that is almost liberated from the repercussions of the expulsion from the first garden. He senses, within the only nature that we know, and centered on the carnal love that we experience, a world gifted with an excess of being, with a new excellence, with a profusion of delights. In the Old Testament, it is he who seeks to give a content to the eschatological vision of Isaiah.

And is it not because of this that the poem reads like a dream? Only an outline of absolute love and of the new earth in a fallen and vulnerable world, subject to worry and sudden violence, the poem consists of a series of scenes passing before the eyes of the imagination, without the coherence of waking life. Thus the many repetitions, and notably that of the watchmen encountered by the bride. They appear the first time with the blur of a dream, when she is seeking her lover:

> The watchmen found me,
> as they made their rounds in the city:

"Have you seen him whom my heart loves?"
Hardly had I left them...

(Song 3:3–4)

They enter a second time, during another frantic search for the lover, as if in a nightmare:

The watchmen found me,
as they made their rounds in the city.
They beat me, they wounded me,
they tore off my mantle...

(Song 5:7)

And thus likewise the sudden changes of place:

Draw me after you! Let us run!
The king has brought me to his chambers

(Song 1:4)

and the inconsistencies, as when the bride who, having lost her lover and asked the daughters of Jerusalem to find him, calmly replies to their question, "Where has your lover withdrawn / that we may seek him with you?" by saying that he has come down to his garden, and that she belongs to him just as he belongs to her (Song 6:1–3). And thus too the sudden appearance of Solomon, advancing with his escort toward his wedding place (3:6–11), or the little foxes damaging the vineyards (2:15). The reader doesn't always know who is speaking, and the translators do not agree among themselves. The reader cannot decide either if this is a single poem or a series of poems, nor, in the latter case, what the number and contours might be. Even the characters seem multiple. The bridegroom is at the same time Solomon and a shepherd, the bride a peasant girl darkened by the sun, the keeper of vines and goats, a "daughter of a prince" (7:2) and the Egyptian wife of Solomon, a virgin (if this is how we should read the

metaphor of the "garden enclosed" and the "fountain sealed" in
chapter 4) and a lover or married woman.

This impression of watching a dream unfold perhaps explains, in
part, the dreamlike repetition of the formula: "I adjure you, daughter
of Jerusalem /... do not awaken or stir up my love" (2:7, 3:5, 8:4), as
well as these words of the bride: "I sleep, but my heart is awake" (5:2),
and these too: "Beneath the apple tree I awakened you" (8:5). At the
end of the poem she awakens the beloved, beseeching him to set her
as a seal on his heart, and declaring the formidable nature of love,
strong as Death and unbending like Sheol. We awaken, so to speak,
at the denouement, when the poet with enthusiasm contemplates
love, the flame of the Lord, capable of uniting beings and renewing
the earth, and which the deep waters cannot quench, or the rivers
sweep away (8:7).

6.

The Song of Songs reads like a dream, and like a poem. Its author
even seems, from the very beginning and in an allusive manner, to
designate speech as pleasing to the senses. The second verse, which
begins, "Let him kiss me with the kisses of his mouth," makes us
think of this maxim from Proverbs: "He who gives a right answer
kisses the lips" (24:26). In saying to the woman, "Your lips, my bride, /
drip virgin honey. / Honey and milk / are under your tongue" (Song
4:11), the man doubtless thinks of the pleasure of kissing her, but the
poet—and perhaps the bridegroom as well—probably remembers
another way of evoking speech, as in Psalm 119, where the author
addresses God with these words: "How sweet are thy words to my
taste, sweeter than honey to my mouth!" (103). The bridegroom and
the bride are each for the other a delightful speech. In a sense, they
see one another as poems. The bride considers herself with the help
of a comparison: "I am black and yet beautiful ... like the tents of
Qedar" (Song 1:5), and of a metaphor: "I am a narcissus of Sharon, / a
lily of the valleys" (2:1). For her, the beloved's curls appear "black as

a raven" (5:11) and his legs are "pillars of marble" (5:15). The beloved does not contemplate himself, but for him the bride's "very form resembles a date palm" (7:8), and her neck a "tower of ivory" (7:5). In gazing at one another, they even exchange comparisons:

> —Like a lily among thorns,
> so is my beloved among women.
> —Like an apple tree among the trees of the woods,
> so is my beloved among men.
>
> (Song 2:2–3)

The poem is renowned for its comparisons and metaphors, which imprint themselves on the reader's mind through their voluntarily bizarre character, by which they both arouse curiosity and create novelty. These figures, the most used in poetry, announce that we are passing into a figured domain, especially comparison, the word "like" serving as the threshold. According to Robert Alter (in his *The Art of Biblical Poetry*), the verbal root *d-m-h*, "to resemble" or "to compare," which appears only thirty times in the Hebrew Bible, appears five times in this short work. The play on words and the highly elaborated work on the sounds of words adds to this impression of a language in effervescence naming a world in metamorphosis. The metaphors especially are astonishing and prolonged. The bridegroom is "a cluster of henna / from the vineyards of En-gedi" (Song 1:14); his eyes are not only doves, but "doves / beside streams of water / bathing in milk, / sitting by brimming pools" (5:12). The bride's teeth are "a flock of sheep to be shorn / that come up from the washing. / Each one has its twin, / not one unpaired with another" (4:2); her belly "a mound of wheat, surrounded with lilies" (7:3).

Far from ornamenting ordinary language, the metaphors and other figures allow the poet, curiously, to speak with precision. The uneasy relation between his language and the real, the fact that words do not reveal things transparently, obliges him to approach what he wants to name in an indirect way. By thus expressing with the greatest exactitude an emotion, an idea, an object, or a being, the poet finds that the *work* of the poetic word, of the imagination among words, consists at the same time in changing everything, in placing the real in another light. The more expressive and right and true the poetic word becomes, the more it re-creates in our perception the world it touches. By being, let us say, exaggerated, the figures in the Song of Songs, along with the extreme work on the words' sonorities, highlight this virtue of poetry, and succeed in entirely transfiguring the world, in order to make the outline of a new earth appear.

A digest of figurative poetry, an exhilaration of figures that jostle one another and branch off, the poem illustrates perfectly the joy of poetry, "this ardor and joyfulness of spirit that naturally excites poets" (Du Bellay, in *La Défense et illustration de la langue française*), and sings the world that the figures transform. It sings above all its beauty—the beauty of love, of creation, of poetry—starting from the beauty that the lovers draw from each other: "How beautiful you are, my beloved ... How beautiful you are, my love" (1:15–16). Reading and listening to the Song of Songs as the word of God does not entail simply distancing oneself from its sensuality by discerning mystical allegories in it. It also entails remaining within the depth of the dialogue, praising with the poet the created world whose center is love, the "flame of the Lord" (8:6), and catching a glimpse of what the poet glimpses. This is how, through the supreme excellence of its subject and its making, the poem justifies its title.

THE POETRY OF THE NEW TESTAMENT

I.

DOES THE New Testament, like the Old, open itself to poetry? It contains neither a collection of poems, like the Psalms, nor a poetic book such as Job or the Song of Songs, nor a prophetic work in verse, such as (among others) Isaiah. The Old Testament witnesses to the many centuries during which the Hebrew people, in reacting to revelations, explored and expressed in every manner possible the nature of God and their relation to him. The New Testament instead responds, during a relatively short period, to a crisis situation in which the Old Testament is fulfilled in a manner at once both foreseeable and unforeseen. First and foremost, the authors recount in the Gospels and the Acts of the Apostles the new Event, the coming of Christ, and its consequences, and they delve into its meaning in the Epistles. With the very probable exception of Luke, in choosing Greek they write in a language other than their maternal tongue. For all these reasons, we might imagine that the New Testament is devoid of poetry.

And yet, it is enough to page through it to notice that, first of all, we constantly come across quotations from the Old Testament, very often poetic ones. As the Hebraic visions and prophecies come back to shed light on the life, death, and resurrection of Jesus, and orient Christian conduct, Hebraic poetry reappears to nourish and transform the new writings, to make them sing. If the quotations allow the authors to give the true interpretation of the Old Testament and to explain that Jesus brings to its conclusion the quest that animated it and the promise that inflamed it, they also recall, by establishing the link between the two testaments, all this poetry that constituted for so long the language properly suited to relations between man and God.

We are so used to the idea that the apostolic authors quote from the Hebrew Bible that we do not appreciate the import of this gaze turned both toward the past and toward poetry. In encountering phrases like "This was to fulfill the prophecy" of such and such prophet, we probe the *meaning* of the quotation without taking into account the verses, and without seeing that what is accomplished—for example, in the preaching of John the Baptist, or the entry of Jesus into Jerusalem, or the fact that at the crucifixion none of his bones were broken—is equally, if I may put it this way, poetry. If we took the time to examine above all Matthew and the Acts of the Apostles, we would become conscious of poetry at the very heart of salvation history.

Given that the authors do not translate Hebrew poetry according to the norms of Greek poetry (not in the Septuagint either), can we argue that the being of a psalm, for example, is found in its form if the New Testament flattens it into prose? But we do indeed feel that the rhythm of the Greek changes in the quotations, and that the words are ordered differently; that the authors listen while writing to the beat of the accents and the dance of the syntax. And we can hear the Hebraic poetry more easily than other poetries translated into a foreign language by the fact that it is grounded neither in the length nor the counting of the syllables, nor in the rhyme, but in figures of construction and, in particular, in various sorts of repetition. These figures stand out in the translation, whether it be poetry or even prose, and I will give some examples.

2.

Next: While the revelations in the book of Revelation are not expressed in verse, the author nevertheless knows very well that he continues the line of the prophets, whose inspired language he uses, and he sprinkles his work with hymns. Nothing is more poetic, and less systematic, than this continual ecstasy, this "loud voice like a trumpet" (Revelation 1:10) telling him to write in a book what he sees and to send it to the seven Churches, or than this "open door in heaven" (4:1) through which the Spirit, having seized him, makes him rise, or this hurricane of descriptions of the inhabitants of the beyond. The sole link in the New Testament to the visionary poetry of the Old, John prophesies on the new present of salvation history, and on the future that is now possible: the final battle, the New Jerusalem, the tree of life from which one can at last eat. A prophet was needed among the authors of the New Testament in order to place all its revelation within divine reality, its true dwelling place, and in order to show us that we lose our footing in this marvelous and transrational world. What inspiration to have placed this book at the end of the Bible, not as some baroque appendix, but in order to complete it!

And during this journey into the omnipresent elsewhere destined to light up our earthly reality, the author continually hears canticles. The entire heavenly company sings, in order to worship God, to give him thanks, to make their joy burst forth, by uttering a celestial poetic word that seems to be the natural language for redeemed glorious bodies. John frequently describes the source of what he hears as a "loud voice" (e.g., *phōnē megalē*, 5:2, 12), which certainly transcends our voices, and he welcomes it in the poetry of comparisons: it was "like the voice of many waters and like the voice of violent thunderpeals" (19:6). Above all he hears a "new song" (5:9, 14:3)—new because the true ode to joy concerns a deliverance greater than all those in the Old Testament, but perhaps also because heaven is the domain of the new, of a sort of eternal newness.

He even hears (5:13) a song that seems to come from the future (or what for us is the future), when "every creature, in heaven and on earth and under the earth and in the sea, all the inhabitants of the universe" cry out:

> To Him who sits upon the throne, and to the Lamb
> be blessing and honor and glory and power
> for ever and ever.

One has the impression that the end of time has arrived, that the work of the redemption of the world is accomplished, and all creatures are offering to God a sacrifice of praise and—may we add?—of poetry.

It is true that modern translators of the Bible each arrange the verses of the book of Revelation in their own way. But let us take the passage where the redeemed "sing the canticle of Moses, the servant of God, and the canticle of the Lamb" (15:3), a striking moment where the canticle that Moses and the Israelites had sung on earth (Exodus 15:1–8) is sung in heaven, and where John reunites in heaven and in poetry the two testaments. Here is the canticle of the Lamb in the Jerusalem Bible translation:

> How great and wonderful are all your works,
> Lord God Almighty;
> just and true are all your ways,
> King of nations.
> Who would not revere and praise your name, O Lord?
> You alone are holy,
> and all the pagans will come and adore you
> for the many acts of justice you have shown.

I indented every other line so as to make the structure of the canticle stand out further, a structure we can detect just as well in the prose of the Port-Royal Bible:

> Your works are great & admirable, Lord God all-powerful;
> your ways are just & true, King of the ages.
> Who will not revere you, O Lord, who will not glorify your name? For you alone are full of goodness, & all the nations will come to you, & adore you, because you have manifested your judgments.

The final book of the Bible is studded with poems, of which we hear at least the semantic and rhetorical configuration.

3.

An even more significant fact is that even the Epistles of the New Testament, which explore the Christian faith from the "prosaic" angle of definition, argument, and controversy, at times change into poems. Some are the work of the author, who in a sense interrupts himself to compose them; others are Christian hymns that the author introduces into his text. In both cases, the lived faith gushes forth, as in the Old Testament, in poetry.

It is not always easy to discern these poems, or to distinguish the exact ordering of the verses, but several appear, curiously, in the letters of Paul, a true theologian and great intellectual. There is general agreement that a hymn is found in his letter to the Philippians (2:6–11). Here is the passage, laid out so as to show the repetitive structure:

> He who, existing in the form of God,
> did not claim the right to be equal to God,
> but emptied himself,
> taking the form of a slave,
> becoming like men,
> and, recognized in his appearance as a man,
> he humbled himself,
> becoming obedient unto death,
> to death on a cross.
> This is why God raised him to the highest place
> and gave him the name above every name,
> so that at the name of Jesus every knee should bend
> in heaven, on the earth and under the earth
> and every tongue proclaim that Jesus Christ is Lord,
> to the glory of God the Father.

Whether this poetic effusion comes from Paul or from someone else, we hear quite well the rhythmic repetition, attractive to the ear and the mind, of "in the form of God existing" (*en morphē theou huparchōn*) in "the form of a slave taking" (*morphēn doulou labōn*); of "emptied himself" (*heauton ekenōsen*) in "humbled himself" (*etapeinōsen heauton*); of "becoming [*genomenos*] alike to men" in "becoming [*genomenos*] obedient unto death"; of "that every knee should bend" (*pan gonu kampsē*) in "that every tongue proclaim" (*pasa glōssa exomologēsētai*). And notice the reasoned precision of the poem so full of fervor and intelligence. The iteration of the word *becoming* underscores, without it having to be said explicitly, that Christ, in stripping himself, abandoned the world of being and, through an infinite descent, penetrated into that of becoming, and that the world of becoming is that of man and of death.

Paul ties this *kenosis* of Christ to the passage from the letter that precedes the poem. In verse 3, he had exhorted his readers to choose humility, and to do nothing "*kata . . . kenodoxian*," "from vain glory." The hymn takes up each of the terms that form this compound word: *kenos*, "vain, empty," and *doxa*, "glory." The vain, the empty, was transfigured when Christ "emptied himself" (*ekenōse*); the true glory appears when all of humanity acclaims Christ "to the glory" (*eis doxan*) of God. The emptiness must be sought not in the futility of self-satisfaction (vanity of vanities), but in the stripping away of self; the glory is not to be sought in oneself but in God. The great story recounted by these few words, tied to one another by the density of the poetic writing, passes from the unreality of a typical human behavior into the immense and astonishing divine reality.

The repetitions with variations are even more numerous and complex in the similarly Christological hymn that Paul composes or quotes in the first chapter (verses 15–20) of his letter to the Colossians:

> He is the image of the invisible God,
> the firstborn of all creation,
> for in him all things were created,
> in heaven and on earth,
> visible and invisible,
> whether thrones or dominions or principalities or authorities;
> all things through him and for him were created,

and he is before all things,
and all things in him subsist.
And he is the head of the body, of the Church.
He is the beginning,
the first-born from among the dead
so that he may be in all things preeminent,
for God was pleased to make dwell in him all the fullness,
and through him to reconcile all things for him,
whether on earth or in heaven,
by making peace through the blood of the cross.

I put together this inelegant translation so as to make evident the network of repetitions, which are even more apparent in the Greek. We hear a synthetic repetition when the words "the firstborn of all creation" come back in the form "the firstborn from among the dead," and when the affirmation "in him all things were created" first returns under the form "all things through him and for him were created," before being completed thus: "and all things in him subsist." "In heaven and on earth" becomes, with a chiasmic effect, "whether on earth or in heaven." The words "through him and for him," in the phrase "all things through him and for him were created," are repeated, with an effective insistence, in "through him to reconcile all things for him." Even the conjunction *eite*, which cannot be translated in English with the same word in each occurrence, participates in this passionate, repetitive, and accumulative song, which makes present the primacy of Christ and his sovereignty over all things without any exception. We hear it in "whether [*eite*] thrones or [*eite*] dominions, [*eite*] principalities, [*eite*] authorities," as well as in "whether the things [*eite ta*] on earth or the things [*eita ta*] in heaven."

The rigorous structuring procedures of Hebrew poetry are purposely loosened in this Christian canticle. The "verse lines" that signal to each other are in each case far apart; the only passage that immediately makes the return of a variation felt, in the characteristic form of a chiasmus, is "and he is before all things, and all things in him subsist." The cascade of repetitions appearing in an unforeseeable way allows us to get lost in the immensity of Jesus's radiance, and supports the reiteration that is the most urgent and joyful in the hymn: that of the word *all*. The image created by this learned writing is both centrifugal and centripetal: we at the same time journey toward unmeasurable distances and toward Christ at the absolute center. The multiple remains and yet is accomplished in the One, and in the end God brings together all things in divine "peace," and Paul gathers all this poetic energy into the peace of the poem.

A last example of the irruption of poetry in Paul is the short quotation from a Christian hymn in his second letter to Timothy (2:11–13):

> If we have died with him, with him we shall live;
> if we endure, with him we shall reign;
> if we deny him, he also will deny us;
> if we are faithless, he remains faithful,
> for he cannot deny himself.

Behind the Greek, one clearly hears the parallelism of Hebrew poetry, for example that of Psalm 19, which I quoted in the chapter on the Psalms:

> The law of the Lord is perfect, it revives the soul,
> the testimony of the Lord is sure, it makes wise the simple,
> The precepts of the Lord are right, they rejoice the heart,
> the commandments of the Lord are luminous, they enlighten
>   the eyes

In the canticle that Paul borrows, the second part of each phrase completes the first, as in the psalm, with the initial "verse" proceeding, moreover, by antithesis. The first two phrases have a happy conclusion; the last two announce unhappy conclusions, and form with the first an antithesis of another sort. The figure of the anaphora—"If we... if we..."—intensifies the form of the canticle and serves to deepen a single thought, like the suite of variations at the beginning

of the verses of the psalm: "the law... the testimony... the precepts...
the commandments."

And it is a twist on the rule that, in the surprise of the fourth
verse, makes a great joy spring up that is both religious and poetic.
The logical thrust leads the reader to expect, after "if we deny him,
he also will deny us," this: "if we are faithless, he also will be faithless."
With the words, "he remains faithful," everything changes, even the
tense of the verb, which makes us pass from the future consequences
of our ways of being to the eternal present of Christ. There, in spite
of our unfaithfulness, he remains faithful, for, according to the un-
expected and astonishing addition, he *cannot* deny himself. In just a
few verses we have a profoundly moving poem.

4.

Poetry resonates above all around the person of Christ. Does Herod
want to know where the Messiah is to be born? The chief priests
and scribes, taking up and abridging a passage from Micah (5:1–3)
that they complete with another from 2 Samuel (5:2), reply to him in
verse:

> And you, O Bethlehem, land of Judah,
> you are by no means the least of the clans of Judah,
> for from you shall come a ruler
> who will pastor my people Israel.
>
> (Matthew 2:6)

According to the first Gospel, Jesus, after being tempted in the
wilderness, begins his ministry by establishing himself in Capernaum,
in the territory of Zebulun and Naphtali, and Matthew immediately
retells the prophecy of Isaiah (9:1–2) that is thus fulfilled:

> Land of Zebulun and land of Naphtali,
> route of the sea, beyond the Jordan,

Galilee of the gentiles.
The people who lived in darkness
have seen a great light,
and upon those who lived under the shadow of death
a light has dawned.

(Matthew 4:15–16)

If we concentrate on the "message" of the text—namely, that from the beginning, the life of Jesus explains the visions and promises of the Old Testament by fulfilling them—we risk failing to notice that it is poetry that serves him as guide. The Gospel of Luke (4:18–19) is even more surprising. After the temptation, Jesus teaches in the synagogues of Galilee and, at Nazareth, he stands up to read and chooses this other passage from Isaiah (61:1–2):

The Spirit of the Lord is upon me,
for by anointing he has consecrated me
to announce the good news to the poor;
he has sent me to proclaim release to the captives,
and to the blind recovery of sight,
to set the oppressed at liberty,
to proclaim a year of grace of the Lord.

Before his amazed listeners, their eyes fixed on him, Jesus declares who he is and what mission he has been entrusted with by quoting poetry. The very first words reported by Luke and that Jesus speaks at the dawn of his ministry are in verse.

Jesus does not content himself with quoting verses; he often composes them, adopting the parallelism of Hebraic poetry as the characteristic form of his teaching. This can—and must—surprise us if we think that prosody and rhetoric have no place in the announcement of salvation, or if we are little disposed, before the seriousness of such a message, to take into account its form. Since Jesus spoke Aramaic, we do not have his own words (a curious fact that would gain from being clarified), and we hear him only through the intermediary of Greek. But, as I have said, we can discern behind the translation of the evangelists the *forms* of Hebraic poetry.

In this declaration made by Jesus, noted by Luke (8:17):

> For nothing is hid that shall not be revealed,
> nor anything secret that shall not be known

there reappears synonymic parallelism, as in Isaiah 55:6:

> Seek Yahweh while he allows himself to be found,
> call upon him while he is near.

Once the ear has become sensitive to this sort of repetition, one perceives it often; for example, in John 3:11:

> That which we know, we speak of,
> and what we have seen, we attest.

or John 6:35:

> Who comes to me shall never hunger,
> and who believes in me shall never thirst.

Antithetical parallelism is heard in Matthew 23:12, among other places:

> Whoever elevates himself will be humbled,
> and whoever humbles himself will be elevated.

as in Proverbs 10:1:

> A wise son makes his father glad,
> but a foolish son distresses his mother.

The synthetic parallelism one hears in Mark 9:37:

> Whoever receives one such child in my name receives me,
> and whoever receives me, does not receive me but him who
> sent me

recalls, among many other examples, the canticle of David in 2 Samuel 22:8:

> The earth rocks and trembles,
> the foundations of the heavens shudder.

Jesus thus prolongs and fulfills the sapiential teaching in brief but numerous passages. And he seems above all to have presented two essential elements of his Gospel in a more elaborate form. When we listen to the Beatitudes in the fifth chapter of the Gospel of Matthew (5:3–10), we hear, even in translation, not only a language worked and made rhythmic through a profoundly simple and joyfully repetitive syntax, but also a language that sings:

> Happy the poor in spirit,
> for the kingdom of heaven is theirs.
> Happy the afflicted,
> for they shall be consoled.
> Happy the meek,
> for they shall possess the earth.
> Happy those who hunger and thirst for justice,
> for they shall be satisfied.
> Happy the merciful,
> for they shall obtain mercy.
> Happy the pure of heart,
> for they shall see God.
> Happy the peacemakers,
> for they shall be called sons of God.

Happy those persecuted for the sake of justice,
for the kingdom of heaven is theirs.

When Jesus speaks in this way to his disciples, we are struck by a
powerful and transpersonal voice, solemn bells chiming in a grander
space than ours, by affirmations that have become familiar but in
reality are quite extraordinary. They stimulate the imagination and
the intelligence by opening door after door. What is the relation
between receiving the kingdom of heaven and inheriting the earth?
Will the peacemakers be called sons of God because Jesus himself is
the Peacemaker in the line of Solomon? With the words "Happy the
meek, for they shall possess the earth," poetic thought draws us
further than reasoning, into a region where we are not sure of recog-
nizing the "meek," and where their exemplary spirituality and its
recompense would seem desirable in relations with others as much
as in reflection and in the arts. (Would not a "meek" philosopher,
poet, or painter, humbly attentive to that which is, receive in his work
the presence of the real?) In meditating upon the pure of heart who
shall see God—in seeking within oneself and around oneself what
such a way of being would be, named with such an evocative sobri-
ety—we can guess that this vision of God is not only a future recom-
pense, but the consequence fitting to purity, lived with an absoluteness
that we struggle to conceive.

And then there is the "Our Father," perhaps the apogee of the
teaching of Christ, which unfolds in a short poem:

Our Father who is in the heavens,
be sanctified, your name,
come, your kingdom,
be done, your will,
as in heaven, so on the earth.
Our daily bread, give it to us today.
And forgive us our debts
as we ourselves have forgiven our debtors.

And do not let us enter into temptation
but deliver us from evil.

This version of the prayer (in Matthew 6:9–13) appears in a series of repetitions that are both simple and varied. One parallelism reduced to the essential: "be sanctified, your name/come, your kingdom/be done, your will," preceded and followed by "the heavens" and "heaven" that fix our gaze, leads suddenly to "the earth" on which these prayers must also be realized. It is a shame that translations do not follow the order of the final words—they substitute a different order: "on earth as in heaven"—for the ample movement of the phrase (followed exactly by the Vulgate) leads to the most humble and *earthly* supplication: "Our daily bread, give it to us today." The words *earth* (*[tēs] gēs*) and *bread* (*ton arton*) touch each other. A more developed parallelism: "And forgive us our debts/as we ourselves have forgiven our debtors," includes a sort of semantic rhyme: *ta opheilēmata hēmon/tois opheiletais hēmōn*, or literally: "the debts of-us, the debtors of-us." The prayer ends on an antithetical parallelism, a true cry of the heart before the glory and the goodness of God: "And do not let us enter into temptation,/but deliver us from evil." The very last word, *from evil*, which can also be translated by "from the evil one," "from the devil," is located as far as possible from the very first word, which in Greek is not "our" but "Father" (*Patēr hēmōn*, "Father of-us"). The words that follow—"For to you are the kingdom and the power and the glory forever. Amen"—take up, in a different order, the glory, the kingdom, and the power of the beginning, by showing that beyond our desire that this *be*, under the gaze of God this *is*. If this passage, considered in our day as a liturgical gloss, is an addition to Matthew's text, we understand that the desire was that the prayer not end on evil, that it be filled anew with the grandeur of heaven, and that after three intercessions concerning God and four concerning men (seven in total, the fundamental number), it uncover once again the majesty of the divine world.

That Jesus often chose not to speak in prose, and to have his teaching follow the norms of Hebraic poetry illuminates with an unexpected light the biblical message, and the very presence of Jesus. It also makes us reflect on the origin, the nature, and the finality of language. The Word, divine language and the source of human language and of the poetry that perfects it, put into operation, while living among us, the resources and beauty of words. And if one prefers to think that the evangelists, in examining various documents, decided on the form of Jesus's discourse, one sees that they believed that the man-God, the perfect man, God on the earth, naturally, at least from time to time, had to speak in poetry.

THE POETRY OF LUKE

I.

To BEGIN his biography of Jesus, Luke chooses to include three poems in the first two chapters. The canticles of Mary, of Zechariah, and of Simeon respond through poetry to the great turning point of history; in order to tell of the Marvelous—the life, death, and resurrection of the Son of God—Luke seems to find it natural to make recourse in the first instance to poetic writing.

He also describes what is at stake in this sudden irruption of the extra-ordinary, as well as the reaction of those who are its actors and witnesses, in a prose that is eminently poetic in how it suggests, through quotations and repetitions, a new reality that it does not make explicit.

This prose first of all evokes the impossible. At the threshold of the story, Elizabeth appears, the future mother of John the Baptist. However, she is barren, like Rachel (Genesis 29:31) who nevertheless bore Joseph, or the wife of Manoah (Judges 13:3) who bore Samson, or Hannah (1 Samuel 1:5) who bore Samuel; and she is too old, like Sarah, who gave birth against all expectations to Isaac, the "son of promise" (Galatians 4:28) and the pledge of the salvation of Israel and of the Church. Luke remembers above all Sarah, without mentioning her (just as he does not mention Rachel, Hannah, or the wife of Manoah). When the angel Gabriel announces to Zechariah, the husband of Elizabeth, that they will have a son, Zechariah replies, "I am an old man, and my wife is advanced in age" (Luke 1:18). Luke returns to the Greek of the Septuagint, where Genesis states, "Abraham and Sarah were old, advanced in age" (Genesis 18:11).

Alone among the evangelists to speak of Elizabeth, he introduces his story through an unsatisfied woman, and through a divine intervention that opens the future by triumphing over the unrealizable. Elizabeth brings together in her flesh all the barren mothers of the Old Testament, and she will bear the last of the old prophets, the precursor of Jesus. From the conception of John the Baptist Luke passes on to the Annunciation, in the course of which Mary, a virgin, learns that she too, although she has not known a man, will become pregnant. While Matthew in this miraculous fertilization (Matthew 1:22–23) shows the fulfillment of Isaiah's prophecy "The virgin shall conceive and bear a son" (Isaiah 7:14), Luke compares it to that of the sterile Hannah. By giving birth to Samuel and delivering a beautiful canticle of joy that Mary herself will take up, Hannah represents the woman whose prayer is answered. Luke's dense and evocative narration vibrates with the expectation of *something else*, of an intervention from elsewhere, echoing the end of Psalm 113, which states as a particularly powerful reason to praise God: "He gives the barren woman a home, / mother joyful in her children," or echoing this prophecy of Isaiah, concerning the city of Jerusalem and the New Jerusalem:

> Raise a glad cry, you barren one who did not bear,
> break forth in jubilant song, cry aloud,
> you who have never been in labor.
>
> (Isaiah 54:1)

Luke begins his story of Jesus with two women who cannot have a child and through implicit allusions to miraculous mothers of the Old Testament in order to suggest that a new era has begun. The frustration of the fallen world will come to an end, a new birth is announced, a new world is born. The words of the angel Gabriel to Mary, "Nothing is impossible for God" (Luke 1:37), which first of all clarify the Incarnation, the humanly inconceivable presence of God in human flesh, resonate through the whole Gospel in the "good news" of the remission of sins and access to eternal life. Gabriel also quotes the Old Testament, God having said to Abraham, in front of Sarah's incredulity: "Is anything impossible for the LORD?" (Genesis 18:14). The Hebrew word means "too difficult," but also "extraordinary," "wonderful"; the Jerusalem Bible translates, "Is anything too wonderful for Yahweh?" Our world, with its rational and material borders that are apparently so fixed, asks only to welcome the impossible wonder. Abraham, too old, becomes the father of countless descendants, and Mary the virgin gives birth to the Son of God.

Neither Isaac, nor Joseph, nor Samuel, nor Samson, nor John the Baptist, nor Jesus is born "of the will of the flesh" (John 1:13). Their births evoke that of the Christian, which is impossible to realize on one's own, as the mysterious language of Jesus shows in the conversation in John: "Unless one is born anew [or from on high], he cannot see the kingdom of God" (3:3), and Nicodemus's matter-of-fact but very human reply: "How can a man be born when he is old? Can he enter a second time into his mother's womb and be born?" (3:4). This is the message of the New Testament: we can be born anew, and the whole universe with us, on the condition that we recognize in advance that within the limits of our possible, such a new birth is impossible, and that, in front of this incredible promise, we are powerless.

2.

Luke's prose, allusive and repetitive, also describes the reactions to this sudden intrusion of the astounding. It creates a very well-defined atmosphere through an effect of accumulation, without Luke having need to specify. Immediately after having referred to Elizabeth's barrenness, he has the extraordinary enter in: an angel appears to her husband in the Temple. Zechariah is "troubled" and "seized with fear" (*phobos*, Luke 1:12). In listening to the angel's greeting, Mary is "troubled" (1:29); at seeing an angel and the glory of the Lord that surrounds them, the shepherds are struck "with great fear" (*phobon*, 2:9). Each time, the angel responds, "Do not be afraid" (*mē phobon, mē phobeisthe*). But the emotion that shakes them so is not only terror at a supernatural being suddenly become visible. It seems to include real dread, a response appropriate to the invasion of the world by the divine. In saying "Do not be afraid" to Zechariah, to Mary, and to the shepherds, the angel separates natural fear, which because they are not threatened they have no reason to feel, from religious fear, which they rightly feel in front of the alterity of God and his messengers. The same distinction is found in Exodus, at the moment of the Ten Commandments, when the people are terrified by the voice of God. "Moses answered the people, 'Do not be afraid, for God has come only to test you and put the fear of him upon you so you do not sin'" (Exodus 20:20). Purely human fear must give way to a fear of divine and salutary origin, capable of mastering sin. Fear undergoes a kind of purification—*phobos* undergoes a *catharsis*. The fear inherent to the fallen world is transformed before the presence of he who judges it and saves it.

Luke explores this fear throughout his Gospel. It takes hold of Zechariah, of Elizabeth's neighbors, and of all the inhabitants of the hill country of Judea when John the Baptist is born (1:65); of crowds who see the miracles of Jesus (e.g., 5:26); and of the disciples at the Transfiguration (9:34) and at the appearance of the risen Jesus (24:37).

This fear is accompanied by wonder. The relatives and neighbors of Zechariah "marveled" (*ethaumasan*), writes Luke, when he announced that the newborn would be named John (Luke 1:63). All who heard the shepherds "wondered" (*ethaumasan*) at the birth of a Savior (2:18). Joseph and Mary "marveled" (*ēn thaumazontes*) upon hearing what Simeon prophesied about Jesus (2:33). Jesus himself, who knows how to be amazed—for example, by the exemplary faith of a centurion (7:9)—elicits wonder as the marvelous become incarnate, alterity suddenly present. The first to listen to him wondered as soon as he began to teach (4:22), reading a passage from Isaiah (61:1–2) on the Messiah. Wonder seizes the disciples when he tames the storm (Luke 8:25), and the crowd when he heals a mute person (11:14); Peter is in wonder before the empty tomb (24:12), and likewise all the disciples in front of his risen body (24:41).

Luke draws attention to this astonished wonder without speaking about it, by slipping it into the weave of his narrative like a sort of leitmotif. Just as good fear makes us sensitive to the power and the glory of he who infinitely transcends us, so wonder prepares us for everything that exceeds us, in an impulse of questioning, astonishment, and admiration. The new that establishes itself on the earth with the announcements concerning John the Baptist and Jesus creates a constantly renewed wonder, and suggests that this ontological affect should always dwell in us. We cannot save ourselves; we need a wonder, a grace come from elsewhere; wonder renders us attentive to this possibility and, once the possibility is realized, keeps us in a receptive state. Through his allusive prose, Luke in the background of his text makes the most striking moment of the revelation of the marvelous take place. When the angel Gabriel declares to Zechariah that John the Baptist "will drink neither wine nor strong drink" (1:15), he compares him to the Nazirites of the Old Testament, and in particular to Samson, who will do the same and whose mother likewise was barren. If we continue to read the passage from Judges that Luke is quoting, in which "the angel of the Lord" similarly addresses the future parents of Samson, we come upon this question from the father: "What is your name?" and on this remarkable response: "Why do you ask my name? It is Wondrous" (Judges 13:18).

Finally, the new world coming to birth brings joy. We already know that *Gospel* means "good news," but Luke engenders joy in the reader through further writing that is at the same time implicit and intense. In communicating this good news to the shepherds, the angel reveals to them "great joy" (*charan megalēn*, 2:10). In announcing to Zechariah that John will be for him a source of "joy" (*chara*), Gabriel adds that many "will rejoice" (*charēsontai*) at his birth (1:14). Indeed, upon learning of this birth, Luke writes, the relatives and neighbors of Elizabeth "rejoiced with her" (*sunechairon autē*, 1:58). The joy is contagious, like laughter at the birth of Isaac: "God has given me cause to laugh," cries Sarah, "and all who hear of it will laugh with me" (Genesis 21:6).

John will also become a source of "joyfulness" (*agalliasis*, Luke 1:14), and Mary's soul "is filled with rejoicing" (*ēgalliase*) in God her savior (1:47). And here is the most poetic and mysterious image of this unhoped-for joyfulness: as soon as Elizabeth heard Mary's greeting, the infant leaped "for joy" (*en agalliasei*) in her womb (1:44). The voice of the mother of Jesus "struck the ears" of Elizabeth and those of her child. Why this image? Because it happened this way? Probably, but we also sense in this curiously intimate and at the same time both supernatural and natural event an attractive depth of meaning. The salutary word is not addressed only to our intelligence; it penetrates our body and reaches a region of being beyond thoughts and emotions, where we are unknown to ourselves, where the child in us awaits birth. Luke thus evokes the secret workings of the voice, like Paul in the letter to the Romans, when he affirms that "faith comes from what is heard" (Romans 10:17). It is speech, spoken language, that touches and changes us, by passing through our bodies, just like the poetry in which this speech is often formed.

3.

At the beginning of Luke's Gospel, an angel speaks to Zechariah and then to Mary, and the Holy Spirit speaks to Simeon. They each respond in poems. These short works, set in an already poetic prose, are preceded, in contrast, by the seemingly passionless prose of a meticulous historian of facts. In the first sentence of this Gospel, which is long and carefully constructed, Luke tells a certain Theophilus of his decision to write down a narrative of the "events that have been fulfilled among us" (Luke 1:1), after having been precisely informed by the surest sources. Once the narrative has begun, he presents, with details that might seem useless, Zechariah as a "priest ... of the priestly division of Abijah" (1:5), and the "practice of the priestly service" that caused him to enter the sanctuary to burn incense (1:9). Everything changes in the middle of a sentence: "the angel of the Lord appeared to him" (1:11). The sudden manifestation of the supernatural creates as much surprise in Zechariah as in the author's prose. In due course, the canticles of Mary and of Zechariah will follow. Turning to the birth of Jesus, Luke explains Caesar Augustus's decree of a census while taking care to note that this was the first census, and that it took place when Quirinius was governor of Syria (2:1–2). Once again, the prosaic language sets in relief the marvelous and the poetry that will soon arise, with the song of the angels:

> Glory to God in the highest
> and on earth peace to those on whom his favor rests!
> (Luke, 2:14)

and with the canticle of Simeon.

The purely informative style continues even after we've read through the three poems, for Luke is keen to fix with precision a certain moment of history, the fifteenth year of the reign of the emperor Tiberius, while naming the governor of Judea, three tetrarchs, and the high priest, before adding: "The word of God came to John in the desert" (3:2). The strange and poetic event, introduced by the prose of profane history, surprises once again—while at the same time curiously appearing in its place, in the world of history thus detailed. This is the Hebrew way to conceive of the relationship between ordinary reality and the extraordinary divine. We saw it in the calling of Isaiah: "In the year King Uzziah died, I saw the Lord seated on a high and lofty throne" (Isaiah 6:1). The same change of perspective is found at the beginning of Ezekiel: "In the thirtieth year, on the fifth day of the fourth month ... the heavens opened, and I saw visions of God" (Ezekiel 1:1), and Haggai: "On the first day of the sixth month in the second year of Darius the king, the word of the LORD came through Haggai the prophet to Zerubbabel" (Haggai 1:1). This way of thinking and of writing seems to emphasize that the entry of the divine into the weave of the habitual is always disruptive, yet the natural and the supernatural constantly jostle one another, whether or not we see it, and can meet within a single sentence. I add that immediately after having named the historic persons in place when the word of God was addressed to John the Baptist, Luke once again brings poetry to bear by quoting the verses from Isaiah that relate to John: "A voice of one crying out in the desert: / Prepare the way of the Lord," and so on (Luke 3:4–6).

4.

The first poem to arise from this prosaic writing that is already being transformed into poetic prose is the Magnificat, the canticle of Mary. Specialists seem to have decided that Luke is taking up a Judeo-Christian hymn, or elements from several sources, and doubtless reworking them before putting them in the mouth of Mary. I am not so sure they are right. They would require us to believe that Mary did not speak or did not sing in this way before Elizabeth, and that the encounter between the two cousins is perhaps to be read as a sort of holy fiction. What is gained by thinking this? And what is lost? It is possible that a pious young girl possessing many psalms in her memory would be able to praise God according to the supple norms of Hebrew poetry. Is it impossible for God to inspire her, and to indicate her words to Luke for him to translate them?

> My soul exalts the Lord,
> and my spirit rejoices in God my Savior,
> for he has looked upon his handmaid's lowliness.
> Behold, from henceforth all generations shall call me blessed,
> for the Mighty One has done great things for me.
> Holy is his name,
> and his mercy is from age to age over those who fear him.
> He has shown the might of his arm,
> he has scattered the proud in the imagination of their heart.
> He has thrown down the mighty from their thrones,
> and lifted up the lowly.

The hungry he has filled with good things,
and sent the rich away empty.
He has helped Israel, his servant,
remembering his mercy,
as he has announced to our fathers,
to Abraham and his descendants forever.

(Luke 1:46–55)

One finds here the heartbeat of Hebrew poetry in the parallelisms. From the very beginning, a first verse, "My soul exalts the Lord," gives birth to a second that brings variation to each of its three terms: "and my spirit rejoices in God my Savior." Two antithetical parallelisms that follow one another—God "has thrown down the mighty" and "lifted up the lowly," he has "filled the hungry" and "sent the rich away"—take the form of a chiasmus (mighty, lowly; hungry, rich), and even seem to rhyme:

> katheile dunastas apo thronōn
> kai hupsōsen tapeinous
> peinōntas eneplēsen agathōn
> kai ploutountas exapesteilen kenous.

This pursuit of form is not merely a matter of technique. The beauty of the verses makes the anger and the goodness of God perceptible; their antithetical and chiasmal tension manifests that of the human condition, caught between the Fall and grace.

Poetry allows Mary to discover and transcend herself. She does not say, "I exalt the Lord, I rejoice in God," but instead, "My soul exalts the Lord, my spirit rejoices in God," because she suddenly discerns the emotions that are within her. Thanks to the blessing of Elizabeth— "Blessed are you among women, and blessed is the fruit of your womb!" (1:42)—she becomes conscious of the unheard-of favor with which she is filled and she feels her joy and her desire to glorify God burst forth. And she turns away from herself, remembering that the mercy of God extends from age to age over all those, like herself, who fear him—over the *phoboumenois*, who have left behind terror of the prodigious unknown for the true *phobos*, religious fear. She identifies with the poor, not by saying so, but by moving from her own lowliness (*tapeinōsin*) to the lowly (*tapeinous*) whom God has lifted up. Whence the importance of an image, that of the proud "in the imagination of their heart." This is probably a way of saying "men with arrogant hearts," "those who have proud thoughts in their hearts," but by translating it in this way, by putting a singular expression into the terms of current English, one loses this vision of the proud gone astray in their own imaginations, in the maze of a fantastical self-image. One loses the real contrast with Mary who, when she looks at herself, sees only the lowliness of a handmaid, and who, above all, looks elsewhere. Her consciousness of self comes entirely from her consciousness of God.

Speaking this way (because she *is* this way), she rediscovers the primitive task of poetry, which seems to have been praise, with her first word: *megalunei*. As in Latin (*Magnificat*), Greek could invert the subject and the verb, and Mary immediately says, according to Luke's translation and doubtless also in her own language: "Exalts." She sings God's compassion, his justice, and his faithfulness to his people. She even identifies herself with Hannah, the mother of Samuel, whose canticle (1 Samuel 2:1–10) serves as the basis upon which she builds her own. She takes up several of its passages, including the first verses: "My soul exults in the LORD, / my horn is exalted in my God." She becomes in some sense other, without ceasing to be herself; her emotion and the way in which she perceives God's interventions do not belong to her, because they are transpersonal.

She also identifies herself with Israel. With wonder and recognition, she affirms, "All generations shall call me blessed," recalling a passage from Malachi, where God announces to Israel, "All the nations will call you blessed" (Malachi 3:12). In her final words, she recalls that the All-Powerful had promised to the fathers of the nation that he would remember his mercy in favor of Abraham and all his posterity, and she understands that it is now and in herself that this mercy is being poured forth, that Mary the "handmaid" and Israel the "servant" are not separable.

Mary's psalm, like many other biblical texts that are both short and far-reaching, represents not only the upwelling of her faith and her astonishment. In order to express everything that is passing through the understanding of her heart, she draws on many texts from the Hebrew Bible, as if her emotions and ideas, while remaining her own, belong to the entire nation and all the faithful. In singing her joy—"My spirit rejoices in God my Savior"—she brings in Hannah, Habakkuk ("I will rejoice in the LORD/and exult in my saving God" [Habakkuk 3:18]), Isaiah ("I rejoice heartily in the LORD,/my soul exults in my God" [Isaiah 61:10]), and Psalm 35 ("My soul will exult in the LORD,/be jubilant in his salvation" [Psalm 35:9]). She becomes language and poetry by welcoming poems that are not hers, because the people of God are one, and because joy, the royal road to God, brings her close to all those who have experienced it. In her ardor, in her enthusiastic story of God's actions, she becomes, like many others, the voice of Israel, the voice of the Bible.

5.

The Magnificat presents itself as a *citational* poem: in almost all its verses we find an echo of one or another of the books of the Old Testament. It resembles the Anglo-American modernist poetry of T. S. Eliot or Ezra Pound; it departs completely from a certain Romantic idea of authenticity by showing that true emotion can be discovered not so much in listening to one's own impulses, but instead in opening oneself to the voices of others. Through its praise, through its *transpersonality*, through the fact that it escapes its author while at the same time expressing her perfectly, Mary's canticle is an exemplary poem, a model, like the Song of Songs, the sixth chapter of Isaiah, or Psalm 148.

The canticle of Zechariah (the Benedictus) comes across as the work of an inspired man, "filled with the Holy Spirit," who starts to "prophesy" (Luke 1:67). If we claim that Luke borrowed this poem and put it into Zechariah's mouth because it seemed to fit him, do we not make Luke a liar?

> Blessed be the Lord, the God of Israel,
> for he has visited and delivered his people,
> and raised up a horn for our salvation
> within the house of David his servant,
> even as he promised through the mouth of his holy prophets
>   from of old,
> that he would save us from our enemies
> and from the hand of all who hate us,
> that he would show mercy to our fathers,
> and remember his holy covenant,
> the oath that he swore to Abraham our father,
> to grant us that, without fear,
> delivered out of the hand of our enemies,
> we might serve him in holiness and righteousness,
> in his presence, all the days of our life.
> And you, little child, you shall be called
> prophet of the Most High,
> for you shall go before the face of the Lord
> to prepare his ways,
> to give his people knowledge of salvation
> by the remission of their sins
> through the tender mercy of our God,
> thanks to whom the Star from on high has visited us,
> to give light to them that sit in darkness and in the shadow
>   of death,
> and to guide our feet into the path of peace.
>
> (1:68–79)

This canticle is also teeming with quotations, and does not concern Zechariah at all, except when one guesses his emotion as he addresses the unexpected "little child." To begin with, Zechariah repeats, with fervor, a recognized formula: "Blessed be the Lord, the God of Israel," which is found, for example, in verse 14 of Psalm 41. In order to thank God for having remembered the promises made to his people, he, like Mary and with the same long vision of the entire history of Israel, goes all the way back to "Abraham our father." He too is aware that Israel's long wait is coming to its end, that a new world is awakening, and he directs his poem to the image that crowns it. This star of light, by "visiting" the people of God, evokes the "visit" of the first verse, in order to show the poem's form, and by coming directly from the Hebrew Bible, it includes within the canticle the poetry of the ancient Hebrew poets. Isaiah speaks here: "The people who walked in darkness / have seen a great light, / upon the inhabitants of a land in the shadow of death, / a light has shone" (Isaiah 9:1). Likewise Micah: "Though I sit in darkness, / the LORD is my light" (Micah 7:8). Zechariah also becomes the voice of Israel. And the image of a great light, of a new sun in the morning, is not simply a manner of speaking, a "poetic" way of expressing what Zechariah could have expressed more directly by saying that God has intervened in order to save his people. By observing through his imagination the light from on high and the darkness, Zechariah goes back to the beginning, when the darkness covered the abyss and God created light (Genesis 1:2–3). He contemplates the fundamental drama, the struggle between light and darkness. He sees in Jesus the new light, just as John sees in the Word "the true light" (John 1:9). He opens himself to the mystery of light, an apparently ordinary and—literally—daily phenomenon, but also the sign, or presence, of God, who "*is* light" (1 John 1:5). Zechariah prolongs the image to the end of his canticle: "To guide our feet into the path of peace." The light that spreads over Israel enters into passing time. A poem vibrating with transcendence does not push aside everyday life, the here and now of the future. The tremendous light will guide the people and the entire world to "peace," the final word of the poem, which clarifies everything we have just read.

As is evident, we learn much by studying the genesis of this poem. Isaiah, before the vision of God in the sanctuary, fears being lost because of his sins, which he locates on his "unclean lips" (Isaiah 6:5).

Purified by a burning coal that touches his lips, he speaks in the name of God and composes his numerous prophecies in verse. Zechariah, seeing the angel of God in the Holy of Holies, does not believe him and becomes mute until the moment in which his tongue is loosened (Luke 1:64) and he composes his canticle. They both know that they are not worthy to speak, and seem to figure the real incapacity of the poet to write *well* unless something else intervenes: an inspiration in the strong sense of the word, or deep memory, the unconscious, an idea of which one had not thought, an emotion that one had not experienced, the hazard of circumstances . . .

6.

The last poem of this lyrical prologue to the Gospel is spoken by Simeon, a particularly sympathetic character whom we imagine to be quite old. He awaits the deliverance of Israel and, perhaps, death. The Holy Spirit has informed him that he will not see death before seeing the Christ. Moved one day to enter the Temple, at the very moment when Jesus's parents come to present their child to the Lord, Simeon receives him in his arms and recognizes, no doubt with astonishment, that the forty-day-old baby is the Messiah. He then speaks the *Nunc dimittis*, one of the shortest and most moving poems in the entire Bible:

> Now, Master, you may let your servant
> go in peace, according to your word,
> for my eyes have seen your salvation,
> which you have prepared in the sight of all the peoples,
> a light to enlighten the nations
> and glory for your people Israel.
>
> (Luke 2:29–32)

The baby of the new world is welcomed by an old man, who can go away now that the future is assured. He is welcomed likewise by

Anna, a prophetess, who Luke tells us is eighty-four years old. Jesus is hailed by a man and a woman from the aging old world who await the deliverance of Israel, as do all of those to whom Anna proclaims the news, so that there may be no rupture between the old and the new. Anna appears in the Bible solely in order to recognize the arrival of the Messiah, and Simeon in order to speak the poem of the making new. Both of them disappear immediately afterwards, like the aged Zechariah and Elizabeth.

Unlike Mary and Zechariah, Simeon addresses God, first of all in order to thank him for having brought him "peace." Thus the beginning of his canticle links up with the end of Zechariah's: Simeon has already found the path of peace that it was John the Baptist's mission to point out. And he sees further than Mary or Zechariah. Mary praises God for having helped Israel (1:54), Zechariah blesses the God of Israel for having redeemed "his people" (*tō laō autou*, 1:68), and this is normal, since salvation comes first to the Jews. Holding Jesus in his arms, Simeon remembers that the Messiah will appear "in the sight of all the peoples" (*pantōn tōn laōn*), and while being the "glory" for the always special people of Israel, he will also be the "light" for the pagan nations. In Luke's delicate art, Simeon once again connects with the end of Zechariah's canticle, the great light that arrives from on high, the fundamental metaphor that links the earth to the heavens, the splendor of the sun and the stars to the splendor of God.

Despite the brevity of his canticle, Simeon is inspired by the Old Testament in both the personal (Genesis 46:30) and the prophetic parts of the poem. He declares that he has seen the salvation of God, having in mind or in his memory, it seems, an oracle of Isaiah predicting that the Lord will comfort his people and all the ends of the earth "shall see the salvation of our God" (Isaiah 52:10). In calling Jesus "the light to the nations," he remembers that Isaiah uses the same expression twice (42:6, 49:6) to name the "servant," the chosen of the Lord. Quoting Isaiah confirms the continuity of the history of salvation, allows Simeon to identify with his people, and makes his canticle both personal and impersonal.

There follows a short passage of tragic prose, no less dense than the poem. Simeon addresses Mary:

> Behold, this child is destined for the fall and rise of many in Israel, and to be a sign exposed to contradiction—and you yourself, a sword will pierce your soul—so that the thoughts of many hearts may be revealed.
>
> (Luke 2:34–35)

Simeon perceives the tragic form of the future: the fall of some and the rise of others, the thoughts that will be revealed as fit or unfit for salvation, joy and misery hanging over humanity. Alone in understanding that salvation will be extended to the Gentiles, he is also the only one to discern the trials to come, and the fact that the woe of the world will be transformed into happiness only through the rejection of Jesus—a rejection so brutal that his mother will be afflicted by it. This is the masterly way in which Luke concludes the poetic opening of his Gospel, with writing that is both precise and allusive, filled with thoughts and images, leaving signs of everything that will follow.

THE EYELIDS OF DAWN

I.

IN THE real there exists another dimension. All religions search for it; the Judeo-Christian writings reveal it; and poetry is its uncertain intuition. The Bible's prose can fully convince us, by its authority, of the presence of another world that informs our own and transcends it. But biblical poetry allows us to glimpse this other world through its very form, through the folds of its complexity, its figures, and all its artifices. For poetry, which is born from the feeling of *something else* within the real (even if this dimension remains, for many poets, in the finite and profane), also presumes that there is another dimension in language. Poetry does not present itself as the most precise and memorable way to articulate what one had wanted to say, but rather as the simultaneous search for what awaits us in the unexplored in language, in the world, and in the poet. To reach it, poetry transgresses the self, familiar reality, and the customary ordering of words, as the poet, filled with wonder, listens to language speaking to him. It is as if language, which is in a vertiginous relation to the Word, already served to suggest that everything in our experience can be open to what exceeds it.

Poetry also awakens the idea of an Edenic language, through the flawless finish of each successful poem. However, faced with the rarity of poetry and the effort and sweat that accompany it, we sense clearly that this language is lost (or inaccessible for another reason than the Fall). Poetry above all elicits hope for a renewed language, and for a new world. In Latin the word *versus*, which comes from *vertere*, "to turn," meant at once "furrow, line, verse" and "in the direction of," and in the word *vers* French has retained the last two meanings. Etymology proves nothing; nevertheless, it is curious that according to this Latin and French polysemy, poetry works the real like a laborer works the earth, and at the same time aims beyond the real as known. Poetry guides us toward the possible in our world while celebrating the here and now of given reality. Biblical poetry plows the earth and opens the sky. And since the alterity thus envisaged appears in part in poetry as such, in the poet's manner of writing, it is advisable to be attentive to this art, to this self-conscious writing, and not to settle merely for signaling that such or such passage constitutes a poem, and mechanically analyzing its form, before moving on to its "message."

Take, for example, a few lines in which Job is cursing the night of his conception:

> Let the stars of its twilight be dark;
> let it look for light, but have none;
> nor gaze on the eyelids of dawn!
>
> (Job 3:9)

The personification of night tells us that the poetic imagination is at work, culminating in the unexpected metaphor of the eyelids of dawn. The beauty of this metaphor and its capacity to command our imagination and our intelligence comes from its aptness: the rising of the morning light indeed resembles eyelids opening. The image is at once both re-creating and real: in spirit we consider a real dawn and at the same time a planetary event animated by something other than the laws of physics and optics. But the image becomes even more striking if we consider it in its context. The passage does not have to do with the beauty of nature. On the contrary, Job, in looking on the abyss of his sufferings, asks that the day of his birth be shrouded in darkness and that the night of his conception remain forever deprived of light. And yet, from this negative emotion there is born suddenly the memory of the progressive and glorious appearance of each new morning, which Job cannot prevent himself from embellishing even further by transforming it with a figure. The meaning of this new vision of the dawn flows from the fact that it contradicts Job's despair, and that from the midst of his affliction there shines a sudden nostalgia (and perhaps a fugitive hope). The original and unforgettable image reveals Job's sadness in front of his inability to rejoice as before in the beauty of the world. If in translation one removes it—if one *explains* it—we lose this fleeting yet profound experience of wonder, and we erase the complexity of what the text says.

Because of this complexity, poetry offers itself as a more exact and appropriate means to speak of God and of everything concerning him. We are not dealing with a system of religious ideas, but with a Person; the Bible does not call upon our intelligence alone, but, like all poetry, on everything that we are. More precisely, it invites us not to limit ourselves to our reasoning alone, but to venture into the fullness of our nature, known and unknown, into the fullness of a revelation. It throws us off balance. Another gravity enters in.

If one fails to recognize the role of poetry in the Bible—and the role of stories, likewise irreducible to doctrines—one risks getting lost. The preparation of every future theologian or pastor should include the study of literature, so that they learn not only how to distinguish among the various biblical literary genres and compare the writings of the two testaments with those of surrounding countries, but also how to read poetry, how to listen to the difference of its language.

2.

Poetry in the Bible warns us of the danger of paraphrase. It thus invites us to consider anew the interpretation of biblical texts. Thinking is necessary; the desire to understand by assembling the elements of what interests us into a whole is natural and comes from God. However, by following this slope we risk building our own systems, inventing our own articles of faith, and stifling the voice of the Bible. In order to ward off this danger, it would be necessary to reflect at length on a passage that I previously called up in a different context. The very day of his resurrection, Jesus on the road to Emmaus accompanied two disciples shaken by the events of Friday and Sunday morning. "Beginning with Moses," writes Luke, "and all the prophets, he explained to them what referred to him in all the scriptures" (Luke 24:27). What kind of hermeneutic does this explanation imply? Did Jesus, running through numerous biblical passages, construct a theology of the Messiah for those who listened to him while walking, or did he open up one after the other the meaning of each passage, letting the disciples take in the many announcements of his sufferings and his glory? The problem for the theologian is to make out the border not to cross, to elucidate the relations of the biblical texts among themselves without leaving behind the particularities of revelation—while realizing above all that we can know nothing outside of what is revealed.

The book of Job was perhaps given to us precisely in order to convince us of the limits of our discourse on God. Job's friends won't budge from their doctrine that in this life the righteous are recompensed and the wicked punished because they are convinced they have read it in the scriptures. And yet, God's anger blazes against them, the poet writes, because "you have not spoken rightly concerning me" (Job 42:7). Job poses anguished and profoundly human questions, but instead of responding to him, God *appears*. The resolution of the conflict within Job, and the denouement of the drama, is this encounter, which places the relation between man and God on another level. God reproaches Job with having spoken "without knowledge" (38:2), and asks him, "Where were you when I founded the earth?" (verse 4). The reproach and the question are poetically linked. God does not seek to crush Job, but to make him understand where the relation between an individual and his Creator begins. He wants above all to teach him the fear of God by showing him not only his own power but also, verse after verse in a sublime poem, the beauty, the variety, and the mystery of the earth and the stars, of the wind, of the hail, of the frost, of the mountain goat, of the falcon, of the "gates of death." We know from the very first verse of the book that Job already "feared God," remaining upright, avoiding evil, and insisting on offering a holocaust for each of his sons after their feasts, in case they had sinned. The dazzling vision of the natural world and of its Creator's majestic government seems intended to seat his fear in a new perception, created by poetry, of the abundance and the living details of our dwelling place—fear being presented in Proverbs (1:7) as the beginning of this "knowledge" that Job lacks, and in the book of Job itself (28:28) and elsewhere in the Old Testament, as the path of wisdom.

It is the wonder of life and the splendor of the world that God invites Job to contemplate. The poetry of God's speeches (chapters 38 to 41) constantly fills the reader with wonder by evoking, for example, the moment when God laid the cornerstone of the earth and "the morning stars sang together/and all the sons of God shouted for joy" (38:7); or by describing Behemoth and Leviathan with persuasive hyperboles, at once hippopotamus and crocodile and creatures larger than life. And wonder is indeed the point. Through his final words, Job recognizes his true error: "I have spoken . . . of things too wonderful for me" (42:3). He finally understands that the answer to his questions about divine justice, of which he knows nothing, is found in this panoramic vision of the marvelous. All our questions are lost in the experience of wonder before God.

God himself, according to the poet of the book of Job, calls our attention to our limits, warning us not to get lost in our own ideas. And if that is very important for the Christian seeking to live his faith, it is likewise important for the presentation of the faith to others. Thus the benefit in reading attentively the passage from the first letter of Peter, considered the basis for apologetics: "Sanctify Christ as Lord in your hearts, always ready to give a defense before anyone who asks you the reason for the hope that is in you, with gentleness and respect" (1 Peter 3:15). From this verse, which "sets the program for fundamental theology" according to Jean-Yves Lacoste's *Encyclopedia of Christian Theology*, whole libraries of books have sprung, aiming to rationalize Christianity and make it "credible." Few bear a title as extravagant as J. S. von Drey's *Die Apologetik als wissenschaftliche Nachweisung der Göttlichkeit des Christentums in seiner Erscheinung* [Apologetics as a scientific demonstration of the divinity of Christianity in its manifestation] (1838–1847), but most have the same sort of ambition. And yet, Peter does not ask us to demonstrate anything at all, but instead to explain the hope that is "in us." He appeals to the life of the believer, to his duty to recognize "in his heart" the holiness of Christ and, according to the preceding verse, not to "fear" those who would make him suffer because of his faith. Beginning from his personal experience, the Christian is enjoined to show why he lives in hope, by announcing what his hope rests in: the saving death and resurrection of Jesus (1 Peter 3:18). Incapable, in any case, of proving anything, his role is to guide the other, not toward arguments, but toward the authority of the scriptures, as Peter himself does in his speech at Pentecost (Acts 2:14–36), and above all toward Jesus, who, far from looking upon the discussion as a spectator, can enter in at any moment through the only persuasion that counts, that of his sudden presence. Peter seems to judge that one is more ready to defend one's faith the more one lives in reverential intimacy with Christ, and I do not know if the translators are right to assume that one must present this defense with "gentleness and respect." The word translated by "respect" is *phobos*, which means in the first instance "fear." Is Peter advocating gentleness toward the interlocutor and religious fear with regard to Christ, whom one necessarily invokes as the source of hope, but must not speak about in just any old way? The "defense" (*apologia*) of the Christian faith and the salvation of the other are serious matters, to undertake with fear and trembling. Since Peter has just encouraged his readers not to be afraid of persecutors, it may be that we are moving once again from human fright to true fear before the transcendence of God.

3.

Poetry, which composes a "meaning" through its proper means, teaches us to respect the text. As I have wished to show throughout this book, biblical poetry suggests above all that everything in the Christian religion is strange, foreign. And this is so not only because it comes from another culture and from another region of the world. It is foreign to what man is, or to what he has become. Created in the "image" and "likeness" of God (Genesis 1:26), he acquired by the disobedience of Adam a second nature, which trembles before that which exceeds his intelligence and his being. In order to approach God, he needs God to approach him through "grace," which can't be forced. Everything that man does and thinks outside this gently constraining and infinitely beneficial influence runs the risk of being false.

And the life of the Christian is strange. At base, Christianity does not ask him to change his behavior, or to obey certain moral injunctions, such as any religion and any purely human system of values might do. It is necessary to love, but Christian love is not to be defined as human love raised to its highest degree. In a sense, one recognizes this, at the least since Pascal's famous *pensée* on the "three orders," which affirms this alterity with unforgettable force:

> The infinite distance between body and mind symbolizes the infinitely more infinite distance between mind and charity, for charity is supernatural....
>
> Out of all bodies together we could not succeed in creating one little thought. It is impossible, and of a different order. Out of all bodies and minds we could not extract one impulse of true charity. It is impossible, and of a different, supernatural, order.[1]

A movement of true charity is *supernatural*; our nature is not capable of making it; if it happens, it puts us in contact with another world. And as Pascal also says, through a fine ellipsis and by substituting, at the heart of supernatural "holiness," wisdom for charity: "wisdom ... is nothing if not from God."[2] *Nothing* if not from God: reflecting on this fact that is at once both known and unheeded helps us to become conscious of the strangeness of Christian life. The love that comes from elsewhere and that imposes itself by grace is the very sign of the new being—of *being differently*—that is required.

The Christian finds himself in a world renewed by the presence of God, in a "new creation" of which he glimpses the forerunning signs. And at the heart of the strange there is God. At the end of the book of Job, God appears under a particularly unusual guise. While describing Leviathan, he seems to speak at the same time of himself. Can you stand up to this animal? he asks Job:

> From his mouth come fiery torches,
> sparks of fire leap forth.
> From his nostrils comes smoke,
> like a cauldron boiling on the fire.
> His breath could kindle coals,
> a flame comes from his mouth.
>
> (Job 41:11–13)

With surprise, one recognizes the already astonishing way in which David presents the God of battles in Psalm 18:

> Smoke rose from his nostrils,
> a devouring fire from his mouth,
> it kindled coals into flame.
>
> (Psalm 18:9)

Seen by men, God indeed appears dangerous—a monster before whom it is fitting to speak little, and well, abstaining from elaborating on one's own ideas, even those of Job, which may appear perfectly legitimate. The fire of his mouth incinerates our theories; his word renders our chattering vain. One should keep in mind this God when thinking of the divine love that saves, of the Father who, compassion itself, "so loved the world that he gave his only Son" (John 3:16). How do we capture in the snares of our language a God that poetry reveals, a God with such dissimilar and apparently contradictory faces?

If the God of the Old Testament is strange, so is the Jesus of the

New, in another way. By declaring, in a formula that will be forever mysterious, "I am the truth," he transforms and exceeds all our conceptions of truth by gathering it into his Person, and he affirms that we know it in him. Whence the strangeness of certain passages in the letters of Paul, every one poetic in the broad sense of the term, and all to be read following closely the very words that form them. They shake the habitual and reasonable representations of religious life. "For me," he writes to the Philippians, "life is Christ" (1:21). The phrase may not be unknown, but it nevertheless brings about an epistemological and existential revolution, the semantic gap between my "life" and "Christ" recalling the seismic one between "I" and "truth." To meditate on these perfectly simple words, asking oneself how the experience of an individual can become another Person, and what this presence of Christ would be throughout one's being and in one's acts, as source, medium, and end, is certainly to discover oneself as lacking in wisdom and far from the goal.

In his letter to the Galatians, Paul goes even further, by sharpening his thought; or rather, his consciousness of himself. I was crucified with Christ, he tells them, "and I live—[it is] no longer I, but Christ lives in me" (2:20). What singular language! The words of the text, without any "as it were" or "so to speak" that one might be tempted to add, clearly mean that Paul manages to live not his own life, but the life of Christ, to be the Pauline variant of the life led by Christ in the whole community of Christians. The Christian himself becomes strange, and overthrows all our theories of the self.

To the Colossians, he calmly writes, "You are dead, and your life is hidden with Christ in God" (3:3). What could be more poetic, mysterious, and visionary! The real life of the Christian is *hidden*, not in the folds of memory or in the unconscious, not in anything human, but in God. It is in a safe place; it is unknowable. Our idea of our self can be only an obscure reflection of our true "image." With these few words, the nature of the Christian's life becomes unfathomable and the medium in which it moves quite simply infinite. It no longer belongs to him, but it is at the same time enriched tremendously.

Just so many short phrases alive with truth, that do not argue, that open doors, that make us feel the otherness of the language of the Bible, that operate like poetry, and are inspired by the greatest of poets.

NOTES

Throughout this book I have tried to make quotations from the Bible hew as closely as possible to the author's French quotations, many of which are his own translations, while others he draws from the translations of the Bible he mentions in the text.

—S.E.L.

STRANGE CHRISTIANITY

1. Blaise Pascal, *Pensées*, trans. A. J. Krailsheimer (Hammondsworth: Penguin Books, 1995), L. 784, 789, pp. 238, 239. (Where necessary, fragments will be identified by the Lafuma numbering in the text.)

A FEELING OF PRESENCE

1. William James, *The Varieties of Religious Experience: A Study in Human Nature* (New York: The Modern Library, 1902, 1936), 414, 378, 447.
2. James, 201.
3. Pascal, L. 160, p. 52.
4. Pascal, L. 427, p. 129.
5. Pascal, L. 351, p. 105.

DRAW ME A GOD

1. Paul Claudel, "Discours de réception à l'Académie française en remplacement de Louis Gillet," in *Œuvres en prose*, eds. Jacques Petit and Charles Galpérine (Paris: Gallimard, Pléiade, 1965), p. 640.
2. René Descartes, *The Philosophical Writings of Descartes*, trans. John Cottingham, Robert Stoothoff, and Dugald Murdoch (Cambridge: Cambridge University Press, 1985), 1:128.
3. Descartes, 2:31 (translation corrected).
4. John Henry Cardinal Newman, *An Essay in Aid of a Grammar of Assent* (London: Longmans, Green, 1895), 99.

5. Newman, 124.
6. Newman, 395, 396.
7. Newman, 105.
8. Newman, 418.
9. John Henry Newman, *Apologia Pro Vita Sua: Being a History of his Religious Opinions* (London: Longmans, Green, Reader, and Dyer, 1879), 169.
10. Newman, *Grammar of Assent*, 268.
11. Newman, 164.
12. Newman, 492.
13. Newman, 417.
14. Newman, 185.
15. Newman, 220.
16. Newman, 132.
17. Newman, 138.
18. Newman, 139.
19. Newman, 138.
20. Newman, 140.
21. Newman, 141.
22. Newman, 147.
23. Newman, 99.
24. Newman, *Apologia*, 198.
25. John Henry Newman to Mrs. William Froude, 27 June 1848, in *Letters and Diaries of John Henry Newman*, eds. Charles Stephen Dessain et al. (London: T. Nelson, 1962), 12:228.
26. John Henry Newman to William Froude, 10 April 1854, in *Letters and Diaries*, eds. Charles Stephen Dessain and Vincent Ferrer Blehl (Oxford: Oxford University Press, 1965), 16:104.

THE LORD'S SUPPER

1. Jean-Luc Marion, *God Without Being*, trans. Thomas A. Carlson (Chicago: University of Chicago Press, 1991), 163.
2. Marion, 150.
3. Marion, 150.
4. Marion, 148.
5. Marion, 141.
6. Marion, 142.
7. Marion, 145.
8. Marion, 146.

9. Marion, 147.

10. Marion, 145 (translation modified).

11. John Calvin, *Institutes of the Christian Religion*, trans. Henry Beveridge (Grand Rapids, MI: Wm. B. Eerdmans, 1989), 4.17.1, p. 557; 4.17.10, p. 563; 4.17.10, p. 564; 4.17.10, p. 564 (translation modified).

THE EYELIDS OF DAWN

1. Pascal, L. 308, pp. 95, 97.

2. Pascal, 96 (translation modified).

OTHER NEW YORK REVIEW CLASSICS

For a complete list of titles, visit www.nyrb.com.

HENRY ADAMS The Jeffersonian Transformation
RENATA ADLER Speedboat
AESCHYLUS Prometheus Bound; translated by Joel Agee
DANTE ALIGHIERI Purgatorio; translated by D. M. Black
HANNAH ARENDT Rahel Varnhagen: The Life of a Jewish Woman
ERICH AUERBACH Dante: Poet of the Secular World
EVE BABITZ Eve's Hollywood
POLINA BARSKOVA Living Pictures
SYBILLE BEDFORD A Visit to Don Otavio: A Mexican Journey
MAX BEERBOHM The Prince of Minor Writers: The Selected Essays of Max Beerbohm
WALTER BENJAMIN The Storyteller Essays
ALEXANDER BERKMAN Prison Memoirs of an Anarchist
GEORGES BERNANOS Mouchette
MIRON BIAŁOSZEWSKI A Memoir of the Warsaw Uprising
LESLEY BLANCH Journey into the Mind's Eye: Fragments of an Autobiography
RONALD BLYTHE Akenfield: Portrait of an English Village
HENRI BOSCO The Child and the River
DAVID BROMWICH (EDITOR) Writing Politics: An Anthology
SIR THOMAS BROWNE Religio Medici and Urne-Buriall
ROBERT BURTON The Anatomy of Melancholy
DINO BUZZATI A Love Affair
DINO BUZZATI The Stronghold
CAMILO JOSÉ CELA The Hive
EILEEN CHANG Written on Water
FRANÇOIS-RENÉ DE CHATEAUBRIAND Memoirs from Beyond the Grave, 1800–1815
NIRAD C. CHAUDHURI The Autobiography of an Unknown Indian
LUCILLE CLIFTON Generations: A Memoir
COLETTE Chéri *and* The End of Chéri
E. E. CUMMINGS The Enormous Room
ASTOLPHE DE CUSTINE Letters from Russia
JÓZEF CZAPSKI Memories of Starobielsk: Essays Between Art and History
ELIZABETH DAVID Summer Cooking
L.J. DAVIS A Meaningful Life
AGNES DE MILLE Dance to the Piper
ANTONIO DI BENEDETTO The Silentiary
HEIMITO VON DODERER The Strudlhof Steps
JEAN D'ORMESSON The Glory of the Empire: A Novel, A History
ARTHUR CONAN DOYLE The Exploits and Adventures of Brigadier Gerard
CHARLES DUFF A Handbook on Hanging
BRUCE DUFFY The World As I Found It
DAPHNE DU MAURIER Don't Look Now: Stories
ELAINE DUNDY The Dud Avocado
FERIT EDGÜ The Wounded Age *and* Eastern Tales
MICHAEL EDWARDS The Bible and Poetry
CYPRIAN EKWENSI People of the City
MARCELLUS EMANTS A Posthumous Confession
EURIPIDES Grief Lessons: Four Plays; translated by Anne Carson
ROSS FELD Guston in Time: Remembering Philip Guston
BEPPE FENOGLIO A Private Affair
M.I. FINLEY The World of Odysseus
WILLIAM GADDIS The Letters of William Gaddis